Jennifer is one great communi _____ ould read
Girl Perfect to help them be ve  nd every
mature woman who reads it v fied with
who they are and how they lo

TERBURN

FOUND.. .NISTRIES

Every woman deals with the desire to be "perfect" and the insecurities that surface when we realize we will never measure up to that perfect image in our own head. With absolute honesty, Jennifer Strickland takes us on her journey through the world of high fashion modeling. As I read the book, my heart broke for seventeen-year-old Jennifer as she was faced with situations no teenager should ever face. As soon as I finished reading it, I went to my own teenage daughter and reminded her that she is beautiful…just the way she is. Thank you, Jennifer, for taking the time and having the courage to write this very important book. It just might save countless lives!

—HOLLY WAGNER
FOUNDER, GODCHICKS CONFERENCES

This is one of the most honest, authentic books I have ever read. Jennifer's life is a miracle, and her message is compelling. The first thing I did after reading the book was hand it to all three of my daughters. I recommend the book, and my friend Jennifer Strickland, to you.

—JIM BURNS, PHD
PRESIDENT, HOMEWORD

Jennifer Strickland's *Girl Perfect* sheds harsh light into the darkness of the fashion world. Jen's story as a young woman intrigued by photography and modeling opened my eyes to the reality of the lives of many girls we see in magazines and on billboards. I highly recommend every girl read this book. Learn from Jen's experiences—successes and mistakes—and read what she's come to understand about beauty, "perfection," dealing with high expectations and demands, and experiencing true freedom.

—BECKY BAUMGARTNER
PRESIDENT, FRIENDS OF BETHANY HAMILTON FOUNDATION

Jennifer writes with a raw honesty about her journey in a world where your value is determined by your appearance. The girl in the picture was beautiful, but her depleted, hollow soul was the price. Deep into her spiral, sitting at a table, she whispers the word "God" and is introduced to the One who could love her deeply and free her from "perfect." Few will ever live in the world she did, but many need to hear her message of the tragedy of getting caught up in a pursuit of externals and missing where true life, joy, and passion really lie.

Girl Perfect is one woman's travels through the empty promises of feminine perfection to a life overflowing with freedom, joy, and the ultimate hope.

An honest, tender, and powerfully written story! Jennifer's voice captured my heart and I couldn't put the book down until I finished it. If you long to be the girl God made, you will find a road map to your land of freedom within these pages. You too can break free, heal, and ride the wave of your dreams! Jennifer is a light shining courage and grace, a role model to women of all ages.

Girl Perfect is an inspiring read. Throughout Jennifer's crazy and ugly experiences in the "beautiful industry" of modeling, she shares how vulnerable and empty it left her and that only God can fill that void in our lives and heal all our hurts. She teaches us that the Lord made each girl unique and that we are perfect in God's eyes if not in the world's. I love how Jennifer wove the wisdom of Bible verses into each chapter. This is an awesome book for every girl.

Handwritten inscription: ♡ KAYLA ♡ — You are SO Precious. Love, JS ♡

Girl Perfect

Jennifer Strickland

CHARISMA
HOUSE

Most Charisma House Book Group products are available at special quantity discounts for bulk purchase for sales promotions, premiums, fund-raising, and educational needs. For details, write Charisma House Book Group, 600 Rinehart Road, Lake Mary, Florida 32746, or telephone (407) 333-0600.

Girl Perfect by Jennifer Strickland
Published by Charisma House
Charisma Media/Charisma House Book Group
600 Rinehart Road
Lake Mary, Florida 32746
www.charismahouse.com

Unless otherwise noted, all Scripture quotations are from the Holy Bible, New International Version. Copyright © 1973, 1978, 1984, International Bible Society. Used by permission.

Scripture quotations marked GNT are from the Holy Bible, Good News Translation, Second Edition, formerly known as Good News Bible in Today's English Version. Copyright © 1992 by American Bible Society. Used by permission. All rights reserved.

Scripture quotations marked NLT are from the Holy Bible, New Living Translation, copyright © 1996, 2004. Used by permission of Tyndale House Publishers, Inc., Wheaton, IL 60189. All rights reserved.

Scripture quotations marked The Message are from The Message: The Bible in Contemporary English, copyright © 1993, 1994, 1995, 1996, 2000, 2001, 2002. Used by permission of NavPress Publishing Group.

Design Director: Bill Johnson
Cover Designer: Amanda Potter
Author Photograph: © Mike Blanchot

Copyright © 2008 by Jennifer Strickland
All rights reserved

Published in association with the literary agency of WordServe Literary Group, Ltd., 10152 S. Knoll Circle, Highlands Ranch, Colorado, 80130.

Library of Congress Cataloging-in-Publication Data:
Strickland, Jennifer.
  Girl perfect / Jennifer Strickland. -- 1st ed.
      p. cm.
  Includes bibliographical references (p.   ).
  ISBN 978-1-59979-343-6
  1. Young women--Religious life. 2. Perfectionism (Personality trait)--Religious aspects--Christianity. 3. Strickland, Jennifer. I. Title.
  BV4551.3.S77 2008
  248.8'43--dc22
                                        2008024878
E-book ISBN: 978-1-59979-540-9

14 15 16 17 — 9 8 7 6 5 4
Printed in the United States of America

For Shane,
because you believed I could.
I love you, always and forever.

Acknowledgments

I've never believed that we go through life alone. But at my loneliest moment, I had no idea God was right there with me. Father, thank you for the bottomless love you have revealed to me through your Son. Jesus, thank you for dying for me, saving me, and setting me free. I love you beyond the reaches of my heart and I can't wait to see you one day, face-to-face.

Mom and Dad: Had it not been for the fact that you let me go free into the world, I would have never discovered the real meaning of freedom. Thank you for your unconditional support even when it has been hard to hear me speak the truth. Your tremendous courage will touch and transform lives beyond our wildest dreams! Thank you from the bottom of my heart.

Linda and Larry: When I married Shane, I knew I was getting a gem; I had no idea that behind him was a vault of treasure. Your faith has often been my guidepost, my rock, and my refuge. I am overwhelmed with gratitude for your sacrificial love, your countless hours invested in us and our children, and your steadfast belief that God has called me to be a voice for him. Without you, this would not have been possible. Thank you.

Olivia and Zach: Mommy loves you with an undying love. Be strong and courageous. Never be afraid to share your weaknesses so that God's strength can shine through you. Remember, there is no shame for those who are in Christ Jesus. For the joy set before him, he endured the cross. You, my dear children, are the joy. You are my joy.

My brother, Greg: At my darkest hour, it was the image of us as children that helped me believe a little girl could find her way home.

Kristen and Kelly: Thank you for believing in God and in me.

Jean and Bob: Thank you for "praying me through." He has answered beyond what we could have imagined.

Tricia, Arielle, and Jill: Your friendships bear the mark of truth; when I had gone astray, you were forever faithful. What beautiful examples of love you are.

Stacy: From one girl perfect to another, this one's for you, sister.

Greg Johnson: You are my agent, but, most of all, my hero for believing in a new writer and a new voice in a new generation. You also believed I could. Thank you for your courage!

Lori and Jim Kennedy: Thank you for all you did to get this project off the ground and for seeing it to the finish.

Kristen Smith, Megan Carter, Wendy Sylvester, Lori Kennedy, and Katie Hickey: You are friends like no other.

To my prayer team: You were heard! Thank you.

Caris, Rashelle, and our Get Real Girlfriends Group: You have inspired me to believe that lasting change and faith are truly possible for your generation. Thank you.

To Debbie Marrie, Donna Hilton, Deborah Moss, and Barbara Dycus—my sisters in Christ who poured their hearts into making this possible—thank you for using your gifts to help a little girl's dream come true. And to everyone at Charisma House: You are an inspiration to those who are afraid to listen to his Spirit for fear of what might happen! Bravo! Bravo!

Finally, for Shane—my prince on Earth, who came in riding on a wild horse: Thank you for always reminding me to live my message and walk in humility and grace. There is nowhere else I love to be but in your arms. You are a living instrument of his love in my life.

Author's Note

All of the incidents in this book are true. Some of the identities have been changed to protect the privacy of the individuals involved.

The photographers chosen to submit photos for this book are in no way related to the photographers who treated me poorly while I was a model. I made a distinct choice *not* to request permission to use photos from photographers who in any way disrespected me. Instead, the photographers whose names appear as credits in the photo section were professional, upstanding people who treated me with utter respect.

Special thanks goes to Giorgio Armani, Tombolini, NafNaf, Italian *Vogue*, *Bella*, Jordache, Sergio Caminata, Marco Glaviano, Fabio Coppi, Zee Wendell, Jim Bonner, and Tony Aquilano, who wholeheartedly supported my efforts to help young women.

Contents

Then, leaving her water jar, the woman went back to the town and said to the people, "Come, see a man who told me everything I ever did. Could this be the Christ?"...Many of the Samaritans from that town believed in him because of the woman's testimony.

—JOHN 4:28–29, 39

Foreword

After I contributed to *Every Young Woman's Battle* with Shannon Ethridge, I realized more than ever that our culture has set a trap for your generation of young women.

In order for many to feel the approval you long for, you must somehow hit an unrealistic target of perfection. Since "perfect" is an unattainable ideal, you are set up to fail. While all of us long to be loved and accepted for who we truly are, your generation is held up to standards that reject them for their imperfections, thus eroding the precious "God-worth" that only he can give.

Eating disorders, depression, suicide, drug use, increased hooking up, and self-hate are just a few symptoms revealing that girls—you or your friends—are suffering from a culture demanding they be something they were never created to be: flawless.

The media, of course, inundate you with images of bodily perfection, trying hard to deceive anyone into believing that perfection is possible and that outward beauty equals inner fulfillment. Photoshop airbrushing, Botox injections, and plastic surgery make the average, "real"-looking girl feel less than beautiful and therefore less than loveable. Too many girls unknowingly ask a ruthless world to satisfy their simple longing for unconditional love…only to be answered with a mesh of condemning voices or a deadening silence.

Girl Perfect is here when young women need it most. It recognizes and sympathizes with the longings of every girl's heart: longings to be valued and accepted for more than their flesh, and very real longings for the perfect acceptance, the perfect image, the perfect dream. In this timely book, former professional model Jennifer Strickland unveils the tricks our culture is playing on girls.

Once and for all, she shatters this generation's illusions about beauty and fulfillment as she describes in gut-wrenching detail the misery that came from being an "imperfect" girl in a world that demanded nothing but perfection from her. Baring the self-hate behind the masks she wore, she reveals the heart of God for every girl imprisoned by standards she cannot attain.

This generation needs to hear from someone who has been there! By finally putting a voice to the faces of "perfection" they see in magazines, Jennifer drowns out the voices with the resounding thunder of God's truth: the best choice girls have is to seek freedom from the chains that bind them. As Jennifer points out, freedom *is* possible on Earth, but perfection is reserved for heaven alone.

This book is destined to shed new light on an age-old issue: we all need love. More than we need the perfect body or the perfect look or the perfect image, we need a perfect love. After all, love is the only thing that will last forever; it is, in Jennifer's words, "the only 'perfect' we will ever find."

You or someone you know needs to not just read this book but to truly take it into your heart and spirit. I pray it will illuminate truths you have never seen before.

—STEPHEN ARTERBURN
HOST OF *NEW LIFE LIVE!*

Introduction

D
o any of you feel pressure to be perfect?" I ask the room full of girls with curious faces. Out of twenty-five girls, twenty-three raise their hands. I want to weep. I want to scream. I want to stomp my feet and pound my fists. Instead, I go into a rampage about how the expectation to be perfect is absolutely ridiculous, and everyone needs to let us off the hook, *now*!

I've known I should write a book about the pressure of perfection, to speak heart-to-heart on this issue with this generation. I've known it, yes. But I've never *felt* it at the core of my heart—until this moment as I see their faces. Their dear, creaseless faces with their wide, inquisitive, and sometimes narrowing eyes, and their hands, raised high and reaching.

"How so?" I ask.

Like schoolgirls who know all the right answers, they can't wait to be called on. The pressure comes from mom, dad, grades, sports, looks, success, achievements, their bodies, their faith; and that pressure is making some of them crazy. It seems they have two choices: internalize and struggle with it, or run away from it completely.

But caught in the trap of teenage bodies, they have to live in this world—they have school, families, and futures ahead of them. So the pressure *is* their reality. Like too much pressure on anything, it seems it could cause them to burst at the seams.

And if they burst, they will crack and leak.

There will be tears. There will be cries. There will be sobs. The masks will break open and the truth will gush out—the truth being, they are imperfect and longing to be loved like that.

This book, girls, is for you. It is my way of holding you while you let it all run out. It is my way of telling you that freedom is possible—how I became free from perfect, free indeed—in hopes that you too will let God break the chains that bind you.

~

As a young girl lying under the covers at dawn, my eyes fluttered open and focused on the collage of masks that hung above the window opposite my bed. Everywhere I went as a kid, I wanted to buy a mask to bring home and add to my collection. I loved the perfection of their smooth, porcelain faces, teardrops painted on slightly blushed cheeks, lips pressed together and frozen in time. When my friends stayed overnight, all those hollow eyes staring back at them would freak them out. "Those things are scary," they would say. But not me; I loved my masks. I found their flawless, unchanging appearances to be…beautiful.

Since I was a little girl running, leaping, and rolling on the emerald green grass that served as the giant blanket of our backyard, I have always been drawn to perfection. I loved to hide in the arching limbs of the massive oaks, play in the trickling stream behind the bank of our lawn, and watch the sun reflect off the water like diamonds dribbling over the rocks. I used to lie down on the warm, tickly grass and gaze at the silhouette of the oak leaves against the incandescent sky. And even though I knew I shouldn't, I always tried to look straight at the sun for just a moment so I could see the light in all its brilliance.

My mom says I always wanted everything just so—underwear folded neatly in the drawers and shoes lined in the closet just right. I wanted every hair in place and pouted if it wasn't. At school, I liked As, not A-minuses, and was prone to crying bouts when I didn't get what I expected.

Like most girls, I liked the idea of being liked. I wanted guys to like me, girls to be my friends, and teachers and parents to approve. At the core of my heart, I wanted what almost every girl in this world wants: peace, love, and happiness. My best friends and I used to write these symbols on our notes, lockers, and book covers: peace signs, hearts, and smiley faces. That's all we wanted out of life. Little did I know that I would travel the globe in search of these ideals in a world that couldn't deliver. It wouldn't be until that world had chewed me up, spat me out, and I had landed at the bottom of myself that I would realize peace, love, and happiness were within my reach all along; they were right there in my own backyard.

Toward the end of elementary school, I became awkward from top to bottom. My long arms and legs got in the way as I ran and played. I wore big, thick, wraparound braces with headgear that indented into my frizzy hair, which grew more like a bird's nest every minute. To top it off, I broke both elbows when I fell off the top of our motor home while playing Charlie's Angels, so I had to go to school wearing double casts and slings. Let's just say no one thought I was very graceful!

Since I was so uncoordinated, my mother tried everything to help me gain some poise—dance, tap, ballet, all of which I loathed—and my dad tried softball, but I couldn't hit or catch a ball coming straight at me for anything, so that was no fun. Finally, Mom heard about a little modeling class at a local charm school, and she signed me up. To both of our surprise, I loved it.

Eventually the braces came off, my hair grew longer, and I grew taller. Modeling school became a world in which I fit—a place where I discovered something I was good at. I practiced standing up straight, walking the T-ramp with a telephone book on my head, applying makeup, and even standing like a mannequin in a store window. For the next several years, while my friends went to cheerleading practices, dance classes, and volleyball tournaments, I went to modeling classes, auditions, and photo shoots.

At seventeen, I found myself brokenhearted over a high school love that ended, feeling rejected and hated by many at school and wishing I could just fly away. It seemed my ticket to freedom came when I was offered a modeling contract from world-renowned agent Nina Blanchard and an academic scholarship to the University of Southern California. Sure that the future was bright and I would have no problem tackling school and modeling, I went off to Europe the week after high school graduation. I was seventeen and on my own in Hamburg, Germany. I didn't want to come back for college; I wanted to follow my dream and go with the other models to Paris, Milan, and New York.

But during some tearful phone calls to my brother and my agent, I decided to return home. The next four years were a whirlwind—working in Europe in the summer, living in Germany, Paris, Greece, Australia, and Milan; and then coming back to Los Angeles for school in the fall, juggling TV commercials, ad campaigns, catalogs, and classes. I grew up fast.

I lived in a world based on "perfect." If I wasn't chasing the perfect affirmation from people in the modeling industry, I was chasing the perfect acceptance from people at school. If I wasn't chasing the perfect body for the business, I was after the perfect grade, the perfect essay, or the perfect score.

Without even realizing it, I spent the next ten years chasing that flawlessness that had so attracted me as a child, as if it would bring me the fulfillment I longed for. Believing the lies the world tells women about beauty, love, and happiness, I went after perfection until it nearly killed me: the perfect size, the perfect shape, the perfect image, the perfect look, the perfect student, the perfect daughter, the perfect path, the perfect escape. Later, even after I left the modeling business at age twenty-three, I attempted to be the perfect Christian. And that carried into wanting to be the perfect wife who ran a perfect house, until that nearly destroyed me too. It wasn't until after ten years of living a life of faith that I finally got it. This is not Eden—there *ain't no perfect* here.

Perfection comes in heaven alone. In surrendering to that truth, we can find freedom here on Earth, freedom from the lies that trick us into believing we are *less than*, because we are *all* less than perfect.

Never once in all my years of modeling did I ever feel that I could measure up to the standards of the world around me. Nor could I ever be the flawless person the business demanded of me—the kind that always looks "just so" on the outside no matter how she feels within. That has never been my strength. My face usually betrays how I'm feeling, so much so that the looks on my face have gotten me in trouble at times!

But in order to make it as a model, I had to learn to wear the masks. And I did. I wore many masks. I wore them so well that even my own parents could not always see through them. When I came back from having quit the modeling industry in search of a more authentic life,

I discovered my mother had a big collage of my pictures on a wall at home—pictures from photo shoots, pages from magazines, advertisements, cover shots.

Angrily, I demanded that she take them down. Naturally, she was confused; the collage represented my parents' pride in their daughter's career. But I knew what they didn't know—those pictures were only masks, and the stories behind some of them were too bitter to even relay at the time.

During the height of my career, while modeling on the runway for Giorgio Armani in Milan, I realized that, beneath the veneer, I had become an empty shell. I literally stepped off the light of the runway into the darkness of backstage life, and it was like a veil lifted from my eyes. I could see clearly for the first time. The beautiful, sculpted faces and bodies around me seemed to hold prisoners within. It is possible that the emptiness I saw in the models surrounding me was just a mirror reflection of the void in my own soul, but what matters is *I saw it*.

I did not want to face it, though; I had worked too hard to get there. Hence, the furious pace of the fashion elite became my own—running from country to country, job to job, from photo shoot to makeup chair to the gym and back all over again. My life took on a momentum of its own, as if I were caught in a tornado from which I could not escape. I wanted to be released from the pressure of it all—the pressure to be perfect—but I had no clue how or which way to turn or who to call for help. I was the prisoner, and the chains that gripped me were really chains I had placed on myself.

With no way to get free, my life spun out of control in such a rapid downward spiral that I didn't even see it happening. Eventually the whirlwind spat me out. When I landed, all the feelings of inadequacy had tunneled their way out of my heart and surfaced on my face and body. I simply could no longer cover the vacancy within.

It was at this time when I was down to mere skin and bones, using drugs, contemplating suicide, riddled with confusion, and haunted by loneliness that I discovered a perfect love that filled the caverns of my heart. It was *the* great discovery of my life: a love that washed over all the imperfections. This love returned me to that childlike state where I didn't care what people thought, and I ran unshackled. The chains that had coiled around my soul were broken again and again, one by one. Love set me free.

This book gives you little glimpses into what my life as a professional model was really like. But more important than giving you a backstage pass to the world of fashion, I want to share with you the lessons I learned along the way. That's why you'll find that each chapter drives home a key principle, and within that chapter I share various experiences that led me to understand that principle and the part it played on my journey to freedom. That means my stories are not always arranged in the order that they happened to me, but rather they are grouped around the topic being discussed in each chapter. A timeline of my entire modeling career has been included as an appendix in the back of this book, and I hope you'll find it a helpful tool as you read on.

Although this book gives you snapshots of the story of my journey, it is not actually about *me*. It is about *you*—that girl inside of you who once ran so free, or at least longed to. It is about that innocent part of you who still wants little more than peace, love, and happiness. It is for you that I write—for that little girl within you on her own journey in search of perfect.

Whether you are looking for a perfect love, a perfect body, or a perfect escape, there is one thing that unites us: we all struggle to find that which will satisfy the longings of our hearts. And deep down we all desire a vast, wild river of love to flow in and through us, to carry us through this tumultuous place called Earth.

It wasn't until my perfect masks fell off the wall of my mind and shattered into a thousand pieces that God was able to put my little-girl heart back together in a mosaic more beautiful than ever before. It is all my shattered illusions that I bring to you in the pages of this book. And it is by looking at the mosaic God made out of the broken shards of my heart that I believe you will be able to see who he originally made you to be.

Are you a *girl perfect* like me? A girl who wants a perfect love in an imperfect world? I believe you are because, as Jack London puts it, we are all made up of the "same nonunderstandable fabric," the same "star-dust and wonder."[1] Yes, we are made of the same stuff, my friend. And it is the same freedom we long for. I invite you to take this journey with me, hand in hand, like two Dorothys on the road to Oz. That yellow brick road may contain some twists, turns, ups, downs, and certainly a tornado or two, but it will eventually lead us back home to our own backyards, where treasures await us…and where we truly belong.

Chapter 1

THE PERFECT AFFIRMATION

Guys and Sexuality

*S*ometimes *you are absolutely gorgeous and other times totally ugly—never in between,"* the photographer says matter-of-factly, his face hidden behind a big black lens. He says it like I am an object, a specimen he is examining in his science lab.

After the shoot he asks me to open my robe so he can see my breasts.

This is not uncommon in Europe. Many times I have been asked to try on a bra and underwear in front of a panel of people. And in Europe, topless girls appear in Vogue, Elle, and Marie Claire (just to name a few). They are topless on the beach, for goodness' sake. So to them, this is normal.

But I am an American. To me this is not normal; it makes me highly uncomfortable. It is certainly not the way I was raised, nor does it reflect the way photographers and agents treat me back home. This is my third stint working in Europe though, so I am used to this.

Stupid girl that I am, I open my robe.

"It is a pity they are so small," he quips as I cinch the robe shut again, regretting it already. "Italian men like women with big titties."

I remind myself that the vast majority of the photographers I work with are simply doing their jobs. Out of ten photographers, nine are nice, professional guys. But as the smoke of his joint twirls in the air, I realize this guy is not so nice.

Launching an airtight defense in my mind, I think about how I had intentionally lost weight before coming to Milan. Having just graduated college, I was finally free to work in Europe for as long as I wanted, and I really wanted to do the runway. I had to be pencil thin, so what can I say?

I fasted from everything: food, alcohol, fat, calories. And I ran like mad, every day on the beach. I guess I left my femininity there on the shore, because there wasn't much of me left. Not that it mattered. I was never a swimsuit kind of model anyway—never had the body for it.

Instantly, I hate the photographer for speaking to me this way. What I should do is walk out, but I don't. I just swallow it, like I have been swallowing things for so many years, putting on the mask that says, "I am strong, and what you say means nothing to me. It has no impact on the way I see myself."

The truth is I hate myself just as much as I hate him. I hate myself for wanting affirmation so badly that I would actually bare myself to this snake. I hate myself that the real reason I went to his studio was for a "test" shoot, to get "beauty" shots for a popular local magazine that wants to use me in their makeup segment—you know, those pictures where you see the girl washing her face, applying concealer, plucking her eyebrows, yada yada. Obviously, I did not expect him to ask me to open my robe and offer me pot after the shoot.

Later, as he drives me home in the pouring rain, his little European car skimming over the cobblestones, I open the window.

"Your makeup and hair will get wet," he cautions.

"I don't care," I say bitterly, pressing my face toward the wind. I want to get wet. I feel dirty. I am stoned, angry, and too far from home.

When I get back to my apartment, I take a scalding hot shower, furiously scrubbing the makeup off. As the beads of water cascade over my tired neck and shoulders, I bow my head and let the tears flow. I want to wash away what I have done. I want to wash away this pounding fog in my head. But, most of all, I want to wash away his words: "Sometimes gorgeous... other times ugly... it is a pity they are so small."

Little do I know those words would root themselves so deeply in my heart that I would feel like a jerk every time the clothes didn't fit right. I would constantly fear looking ugly if I turned the wrong way, and I would end up going from person to person in Milan, looking for that stamp of approval that I thought would validate me.

For now, standing under the spray of the hot shower, I just try to wash it away. Then I can get up the next day, put on the mask again, and pretend the things they say about me don't bother me in the least.

What We're Really Longing For

Affirmation: *to validate, confirm; to state positively; to assert, to express dedication to*

The world tells us that our affirmation comes from men. If a man tells you that you are beautiful, it is so. If a guy tells you that you are intelligent, it is so. If he is attracted to you, then you are worthy. You are validated. On the other hand, if a man says you are not dateable, not pursuable, or that you are ugly, stupid, or unlovable, then this is what you come to believe.

To take it even further, the world claims our value comes from our sex appeal. In other words, if we are sexy, we are *it*. We are the *bomb*. If we are not, then we really aren't worth much.

It's a fact that in our society, young girls feel pressure to look older and sexier. The first time I ever remember sensing this, I was about ten years old. I arrived at the hotel, holding my auntie's hand. As I scanned the pool, draped with long-legged models wearing high heels and swimsuits, photographers fawning over them, I felt instantly inadequate. The models' bikinis were filled with cleavage and rounded hips. As they emerged from the water, it clung in little beads to their oiled, suntanned skin. They were so made up, so womanly.

But the photographer seemed fine with the fact that I was a *kid*. First, he placed me in front of a waterfall, posing with a giant stuffed lion. But when he took that away and I stood there in my rainbow-striped swimsuit that stretched over my chest flat as a pancake, I felt suddenly embarrassed by the fine white hairs on my legs, my girlish body, and my inability to be sexy.

Later, he had me climb a tree and look down at the camera for a close-up. "Amazing!" he exclaimed. "You look eighteen years old here! Perfect, perfect." Then *snap, snap, snap* went the shutter.

There it was. They would applaud me when I looked like a woman, when I was sexy, when I looked older than I was, and when I was something that, at the moment, I really was not.

While you may not have been standing in front of a camera as I was, you've probably experienced similar feelings of embarrassment as you compared yourself to more physically mature girls or young women. It's a fact of life that girls get validated for looking older than we are—at least until we hit our thirties when society starts telling us we should look younger! But, that aside, when it comes to girls, the world tends to be in a rush to make them into women.

In turn, as girls responding to the world we live in, looking for validation and hungry for affirmation, we are in a hurry to get curves, get our periods, become dateable and pursuable. Then we must get married, have children, have the best-looking house, and the list goes on and on. Why? Because we want to be stamped as being good enough, beautiful, or even better, perfect.

 Deep inside I was really just a schoolgirl who wanted someone to applaud me, someone to tell me that I did a good job or that they loved me!

A Quick Word About My Parents

Before I go any further into these stories, I must make a disclaimer about my parents that stands for the entire book: they knew very little about what really went on behind the scenes in the modeling industry. There were three reasons for that.

First, they were naïve and uneducated about the business. Second, they were in denial—they did not want to believe that anyone would try to take advantage of their little girl—and so they did not ask about details. They considered my modeling opportunities to be rare and exciting, and simply said, they wanted me to succeed. Third, I never told them about what went on behind the scenes. If I had, maybe I would have gotten a ticket out of the business early on.

It might help to understand that my mother was raised in a family that didn't allow her to pursue big dreams for her life, so the last thing she wanted to do was squelch my dreams. She wanted me to experience things she never had a chance to even consider for herself. Both she and my father were raised in homes where they just didn't communicate well. At least there was very little *honest* communication about the hard stuff. There was a type of code of silence inherited in their generation, and they were taught *not* to talk about matters that were believed to be private.

Our home was very loving and very moral. My parents loved me deeply, and still do. I do believe, however, that they made some very poor choices in not protecting me more or keeping in closer communication with me about the situations I found myself in. But at the time, I wanted success as much as they wanted it for me, so I wore those masks that kept them from seeing the truth.

On top of it all, my agent Nina Blanchard had an incredible reputation for integrity, and rightly so. She was, and is, very well thought of and highly respected in the industry, and she always assured my parents that the agents in international countries would go to great lengths to take care of me. I lived in Nina's Hollywood mansion with her for a summer and the truth is, she watched over us models like a hawk. But when it came to the foreign agents, this was a total farce.

My agents throughout Europe let the models go anywhere and do anything we pleased. And they never said a word about our lifestyle choices as long as we showed up looking pretty for work.

When it came to my first photo shoot, Mom wanted to go with me, but that just wasn't *chic* in the business and so I refused her. I was seventeen years old and extremely strong-willed, and I just bowled over her with what I wanted to do.

Time and time again, Mom and Dad let me go alone to Europe. My folks used what they believed was conventional wisdom toward me: she has a good head on her shoulders; she gets straight As; she's smart; she'll be fine.

If you ask my mother today if she would do that again, her eyes would fill with tears, her face would crunch up, and she would say, "Absolutely not! No, never. Never, never, never! I should *never* have let her go alone!"

But that was then, and this is now.

Not only does the world tell us our validity stems from our sex appeal, but it also expects us to exercise that sexuality—regardless of whether we can handle the repercussions of becoming sexually active. The very day I signed a modeling contract with the Nina Blanchard Agency, Nina sent me to a Hollywood photographer to see how I moved on film.

The photographer told me to bring a short, tight black dress that showed my body, black sheer stockings, and black pumps, as well as anything else I wanted to wear. When I got to his apartment, he showed me a corkboard tacked with snapshots. Pointing to a picture of a woman wearing a little black dress, standing with her legs straddled, and fists clenched as if she were about to punch someone, he told me to, "Play with that mood."

I looked at the woman in the picture—and she was a *WOMAN*; with big, firm breasts, muscular legs, and a look of hard-fought confidence in her eyes—and I thought to myself, "I don't even have that 'mood' in me!" I was just a *GIRL* from a simple town with simple ways. I didn't feel I could have this magnetic power on film, this gripping sexuality. But that is what he wanted. Of course, with my desire to please, I told him I would try my best.

We took a few shots on his rooftop and stairwell, and then he told me to put on the little black dress. As he led me down the sidewalk outside his apartment, some guys whistled from across the street. With my torso painted in the cold, black cotton, legs propped in stockings and high heels, and hand in hand with the photographer—who was twice my age—I felt like a prostitute. I kept telling myself that I was a model, not a whore, and there was a difference.

This was a battle that would continue to wage in my head for the next six years, as countless men dressed me up however they pleased and took my picture. No, I never even came near to selling sex as prostitutes do. In fact most of my work was very all-American: Eddie Bauer, Jordache, Oil of Olay, and so on.

When I look back, however, I realize that I allowed my face and body to be bought and sold for a price. It was used for whatever they were trying to sell at the moment—clothes, cars, makeup—and then cast away when they were done with it, or when another, prettier girl came along. While this might not be the least bit disturbing for some models, for my little girl's heart, it was.

But on the sidewalk that day in Hollywood, I was still clueless as to what that photographer was trying to do when he placed my back against the wall, gently pulled my arms away from my body, and brushed my soft, blonde curls off my shoulders so they cascaded down my back. Backing into the street with his camera in hand, he told me to imitate the girl in the picture he had shown me—look angry, sexy, sassy.

Crouching in the middle of the street, shooting the camera up at me as I kept giggling and falling back against the wall, he continued telling me to get tougher, meaner, straddle my legs a little more, and a little more, and still a little more…and following his cues, I did. Wrapping my arms around my back, leaning forward on one pump, and glaring down the chute of the camera, past the one who took the pictures, I dove into the lightlessness that existed there. I dove right into that world.

It would be a long and twisted tunnel. While I was still young and innocent, they were trying to draw the sexuality out of me. It took a long time for me to realize that, in this world, sex is money…sex is power…sex is what they want.

As you might imagine, it got much darker and more dangerous in the coming years because I was constantly in situations where I was alone with men much older than I. The men were usually very careful to make everything look innocent on the outside, but inside many of them wanted something else.

After graduating college at twenty-one, I signed with Ford Models New York and Fashion Model Management in Milan and went off to Italy to do magazines and runway. I was only in the country a few days when I did a six-page spread for a popular magazine. In the pictures, I wore plaid skirts, white blouses and suspenders—a classic schoolgirl's uniform.

The clients wanted me to be young and energetic, so I spent the day smiling, leaping, and even dancing on stage in front of the camera. They decided to give me the cover of the magazine, and at the end of the day, the crew actually applauded for me—I think it was the one and only time that ever happened!

After the shoot, I was walking down a dimly lit hallway toward the exit of the building. No one was around. Feeling great about the day's work, I had my bag slung over my shoulder and a little skip in my step. Then, out of the blue, I felt someone's strong hand grip my forearm. Stunned and terrified, I swung around and faced a man whom I had seen on the set of the day's shoot. He had snuck up on me. The deeply embedded lines of his face seared themselves in my memory. The hallway behind him was long, empty, soul-less.

I tried to ask him what he wanted, and although he spoke no English, he showed me in gestures that he wanted me to have sex with him. The man was at least ten years older than my father!

Revolted by the very thought of it, I attempted to pull away, but he squeezed my arm tighter. With the full force of my body, I yanked myself away from him and raced down the hallway, panicking to find an open door. I pushed on the first one I saw and it opened. Glancing back, I saw his silhouette as he stood immobile in the hallway. I ran down the stairs and into the street.

Once outside in the dark, I hurried all the way to the metro, my heart pounding. Then on the train, I kept my head down; I didn't want anyone to see how shaken I was. Scuffling along the dim street to my apartment, I finally came to my door, fiddled with the lock, pushed it open, slammed it shut, and locked it. The next thing I did was jump in the shower and try to wash it all off.

 The world claims to appreciate innocence, to believe in its purity and beauty, and at the same time it can't wait to snatch it away.

Even now, every time I see those pictures, I see that man's face. In the pictures from that day's shoot, I look happy and free, young and innocent. Deep inside I was really just a schoolgirl who wanted someone to applaud me, someone to tell me that I did a good job or that they loved me! But to that man, my affirmation would only come from pleasing *him*.

This is how our world views girls and sexuality. And there are so many more instances like this one that I could share with you. But this next story shows just how low it got—how wicked, convoluted, and deceitful some men's desires can become.

The first week I got to Milan, I did a test shoot with a photographer that went really well. I got some pictures for my book and he reported good things about me back to the agency.

A few weeks later, he requested that I come back.

This time, without my knowledge, he arranged for my booker and the owner of the studio to come by and watch the shoot.

That morning when I woke up, I had a big pimple on my left cheek, and I knew the photographer was not going to be happy.

When I arrived on the set, I sat down in the makeup chair and closed my eyes—surrendering my skin to the makeup artist. After an hour of transforming my face, he began to hot glue fake eyelashes on me, one by one, continually, "accidentally," getting the glue in my eyes. I tried to be tough, but by the time he was done my eyes were beet red and the mascara was running. Then, he started crimping my hair.

"You're crimping my hair?" I questioned.

He muttered something to the photographer in Italian, and the photographer tried to assure me that crimping was the new thing—hadn't I seen Claudia Schiffer in her crimped hair on this month's cover of *Vogue*?

"Uh, no." I thought, "I don't really care what Claudia Schiffer looks like on the cover of *Vogue*! I look like an idiot right now." My skin was as pale as bone china; my eyes were bloodshot and highlighted in yellow eye shadow; my hair looked like a shingled roof; and I resembled a sick, deranged Barbie doll. I looked *nothing* like myself. But of course I could say nothing—I had to do my job.

I asked if I could get dressed, hoping that the clothes would help the situation. But to my surprise, there was no stylist on the shoot. I hated working on jobs where there were no stylists, where they just wanted to "throw something together." It just was not professional.

"There are no clothes?" I asked. "What is this?"

"Relax, *bella*," the photographer said, showing me some pink mesh material that they intended to wrap around my body.

Now many of you might be thinking, this is the point where I should have walked out. Good thought. But you must understand, I was a model. This was my job. And I had the eyes of my agent watching me.

So as they stapled the fabric around my bare body, I held myself with as much grace as possible, making sure I was fully covered. They had me climb a ladder, took a few shots, and then lit up the joints.

As they got higher and higher, they had me sit down and pose on a white bed.

I tried, but I felt really awkward.

The photographer huffed and puffed about having to change the lighting because of my pimple. Then, when the set was ready, he climbed to the top of the ladder and shot the camera down on me.

"Lie down," he said, and then after a while, "Act like you are having sex with a man."

With him hovering over me on the ladder and the other men poised around the room watching me with their arms crossed, I felt like a small animal circled by a pack of coyotes stalking their prey.

I writhed and squirmed under the glaring lights. I didn't feel sexy at all. I felt awkward and critiqued and under a microscope, like a stick figure doll that couldn't muster a feeling of sensuality no matter how hard she tried. I simply could not do it—and I told them so.

One by one, they lost interest and began to back away.

When the shoot was over I couldn't wait to get out of there. As I walked through the exit, the photographer was biting into a thick roast beef sandwich, the juice dripping down his chin. He hardly even looked up at me.

"Oh, *ciao, bella*," he said, waving at me as if to say, "You can go now, we're through using you."

I knew I didn't meet their expectations, and I didn't care. I just wanted to forget about it, wash off the makeup, wash off the words, wash it all away.

That weekend I needed desperately to get away from Milan. I had a job in Venice the coming week, so I decided to go early, as I had always loved Venice and wanted to see it again—I had once been there with my family on a childhood trip. Damien, a French magazine publisher who had decided to become my manager in Europe, forbade me to go alone, so he set it up for his son to be my guide and ensure my safety.

While we waited for the train, Damien's son said, "I heard about your shoot yesterday."

"You did?"

"Do you remember that window on the right side of the room?" he asked.

"Yes."

"Do you know that they set those shoots up for girls, the ones with no clothes and no stylists, and there are men on the other side of the window watching you while they are smoking their cigars. They want to see how far they can get you to go on that white bed so they can get off on you. They do it to all the new girls. It's just how they do things here."

He took a big drag off his cigarette. He was a photographer. He knew what he was talking about.

I felt like I had been punched in the stomach. Even though I had spent four summers modeling in Europe by now, nothing like this had ever happened to me before.

"By the way," he continued wryly, "do you really think you are going to get a man like this?"

"Like what?" I asked.

"Like this! Look at you!" he said, mocking me. "You are so skinny. Do you think that will attract a man? You don't even look like a woman anymore."

At that moment, I was not a person; I was a thing. A thing they had used for their own entertainment, their own pleasure. A thing put under a microscope that they discarded when it no longer pleased them. I was no one's daughter, no one's sister, no one's friend. I was nothing but a thing in a world of things, and my only affirmation came from being "sexual."

At first, the men in the business were intrigued by my innocence; they loved the angelic hair, the porcelain skin, the awake and shining eyes, the pure smiles, and the easy laughs. Then they wanted to draw the sexuality out of me, they wanted to find the woman within the girl, and finally, they wanted a piece of her. They wanted to *take*. Over the years, I began to feel like I had to constantly defend myself from them, until finally I was so exhausted I could hardly fight anymore.

So maybe that shoot when I was ten years old was the beginning of the loss of my innocence—that moment when I found out what they would ultimately want from me: sex. If my auntie had known then that this business would eventually swallow her little niece alive, she would have marched me straight home and told my mother, who happened to be ill in bed at the time, that there would be no more of this. Mom would have said, "OK. That's it." But how could they have known?

 Shame continues to steal and steal again until the eyes no longer hold any light, the laughter is long gone, and freedom is only a thing in dreams.

That very weekend, Damien's son—sent along to protect me—took advantage of me for *his* own pleasure.

I was falling asleep in a bed at the hostel when he climbed into the bed, uninvited.

"*No, no, no!*" I kept saying as he writhed on top of me. "*Stop, stop!*"

But he didn't stop. I knew that he could hear me, but he did not listen. He wanted what he wanted. And I had become so weak that my voice was drowned out by his groans.

My soul left my body lifeless. I felt like I disappeared. That little girl who once ran free was dead now, vacant, absent completely.

The world claims to appreciate innocence, to believe in its purity and beauty, and at the same time it can't wait to snatch it away. Once the fascination and intrigue wear off, the world moves on to rob someone else of her innocence.

We girls are left to carry the shame, whether we were responsible for what happened or not. And the shame continues to steal and steal again until the eyes no longer hold any light, the laughter is long gone, and freedom is only a thing in dreams.

Today I believe the loss of my innocence was the worst part. If not only a physical rape, it was certainly a slow, stripping, mental, emotional, and spiritual rape.

That was truly the end of my beginning, and the beginning of my end.

FROM MY WORLD TO YOURS

Certainly, these things don't only happen in the modeling industry. My experiences are simply a mirror reflection of the values upheld by the world. In high school, college, and beyond, innocence is not considered "hip." Girls who are "hip" are girls who are sexual. They dress sexily, their bodies are sexually developed, and, more often than not, they are busy exercising that sexuality.

Of course there is a very fine line between being called "hip" and being called "slut." "Hip" means that you have sex, but not too much and not with too many. "Slut" means you have been found out—you sleep around and people talk.

In my high school and college, you were a very unusual girl if you were not having sex. Sex was just another way to show affection. Sex was a way to be validated by a guy. Sex was a way to show that you were no longer a little girl, you were a woman. If a guy said he loved a girl—and certainly if she loved him back—she was supposed to have sex with him. That was the expectation and the norm. At the other end of the spectrum, it was also not unusual for girls to have sex with more than one guy. After the first time, it was easier for them to go from guy to guy to guy. These girls either went through a lot of breakups, or they slept with whomever paid attention to them.

Here is the truth: girls who have sex with someone they love and girls who have sex with guys they hardly even know—the hip girls and the sluts—are actually looking for the same thing. Both sets of girls have the exact same longing in their hearts, and that longing is for love—affirmation, acceptance, approval, and affection. Every girl in the world is looking for a perfect affirmation—she is looking for someone to say, "I adore you. I love you to the moon and back. I approve of you, just like you are right now. I accept you like this, and I want to shower you with my affection."

Oddly enough, our world teaches that sex is a way to get that affirmation, but actually it's a lie. It backfires. If you go from guy to guy to guy, your longing is never satisfied. You end up feeling rejected, used, hated, and dirty; like a *thing* in a world of things. You become more starved for love than ever, and your level of shame feels bottomless.

On the other end, if you fall deeply in love and give him everything (not talking about marriage here), you end up losing more of yourself than you had to begin with. At fifteen, I fell in love with a hypnotically cute, sixteen-year-old boy at school. We became best friends, and I did what I thought you were supposed to do when someone loved you inside and out—I poured my heart, strength, soul, and, eventually, body into the relationship.

What a roller-coaster ride. If I wasn't in fear of getting pregnant or contracting a sexually transmitted disease from his former partner, then I was in fear of the relationship falling apart and him walking off with my heart. When he was "loving up" on me with his attention and affection, I was happy. When he was pouring that friendship and flirtation out on some other girl, I was miserable, insecure, depressed, and in fear of losing him. I expected him to fill the longings of my heart— the longing for unconditional acceptance and a love that never leaves you. But he was only a boy; he could not fill that place of longing inside me.

Sometimes I found myself laying my head on his chest and just letting the tears roll.

"Why are you crying?" he would ask.

"I don't know," I whispered. "I don't know."

But now I know. My innocence was lost and I could not get it back. I could not figure out why this boy, this relationship, did not fill the emptiness in my heart. I thought that by giving him everything, I would *gain*; but there was something I could not touch upon that was irreparably lost.

After four years of ups and downs, the relationship ended, and I just sank. In the mornings, I would lie in bed, buried beneath the sheets, my body heavy as if draped in chains. I no longer wanted to get up for school; I didn't want to get up for anything. I just wanted to cry—and cry and cry and cry—until my hair was soaked wet with the tears.

Even while I was eighteen and working as a model in Paris, I would lie under the covers while the rain hammered against the window-panes, and I would let the tears run. I could hear the chatters of the models in the next room, but I did not want to join them. Instead, I lay in bed and read books about Buddhism, trying to find some kind of peace.

I didn't care about the modeling interview that day or the party going on that night. I cared about being loved, and my heart felt like it was tearing apart. I kept trying to let go, as the books told me to do; to experience the no-need, no-desire part of Buddhism that drew me to it. I felt that the books claimed that "not needing" anything would free me from suffering and would bring me peace.

Every girl in the world is looking for someone to say, "I adore you. I love you to the moon and back. I approve of you, just like you are right now."

But it didn't work. The more I wanted to *not need* or *not want*, the more I needed and the more I wanted, and the more I longed for something to fill the hole in my soul.

I ended up in the same situation in college because the emotional need to be filled didn't go away—and I thought a man was supposed to fill it. I thought that meeting my prince charming was supposed to be the beginning of my happily ever after. But it was just the opposite; my college "love" was another roller-coaster ride that left me heart-broken, crying under the covers, miserable, angry, and wanting a love that didn't run out.

That breakup left me in far worse shape than the first. My happiness had once again been tied up in a guy, and the guy could not deliver. Then, one day, the guy—and my happiness—were gone.

I knew I was more than my body. I knew I was more than my sexuality. I believed that I had a lot more to offer the world than just my *flesh*! I had heard the "Say No!" campaign. In sex ed class, I had seen pictures of pregnancy, genital warts, condoms. Goodness, everyone in school knew we were supposed to say no. But what I didn't know, what I didn't understand, was, why not? I didn't have a clue what my value was in a spiritual sense.

Many years later, coming to faith in God and studying the Bible for the very first time, I discovered the "why not." First John 3:1 says when we put our faith in Christ, God *lavishes* us with his incredible love by calling us his children. We're his daughters! (See also John 1:12.) God wants us to "know and rely" on the depth of love he has for us (1 John 4:16).

I realize that you may not believe in the Bible, but I ask you to give it a chance. Its wisdom transformed my life and gave me spiritual principles to stand on. Most of all, it continues to be my bottomless source of guidance in a world that has too many otherwise confusing messages to stand on.

Biblically speaking, your value has absolutely *nothing* to do with how men see you or your sexuality. It has to do with the fact that God knit you together in your mother's womb—he created you (Ps. 139:13). Therefore you are the precious work of his hands and the beloved, cherished daughter of his heart. When the Bible says "the love of God has been poured out in our hearts," God is telling you that *he* wants to be the source of your affirmation, the source that fills your longing, so you don't look for that affirmation by sharing your sexuality before you are married. Simply put, God wants to protect your sexuality so it doesn't lead you down roads of heartache.

Your sexuality is not a bad thing; it's not shameful. Genesis says God called his creation good, so the sexuality he wove into your body—used in the way he says to use it—is also good (Gen. 1:27–31). When Adam and Eve first had sex, there was no shame in the Garden of Eden (Gen. 2:24–25). "Shame" didn't enter the scene until Satan, in the form of a snake, convinced them not to listen to God's one simple rule; then, the

Bible tells us, they were naked and ashamed (Gen. 3:7–8). The shame came from disobeying God. Instead of seeing his rule as a boundary to protect them, they saw it as too confining.

It wasn't the sexuality that was shameful; it was the disobedience.

But just because sexuality isn't a bad thing, that doesn't mean it is something to be used to receive affirmation. As you can see in my situation, it didn't fill my longing to be validated; instead, it left me longing even more for *real* love that wouldn't hurt me.

God's Word—which never changes no matter how cultural norms change—continues to define sex as something to unite married couples and bring forth children. Of course, our world today accepts having sex almost as freely as it does a good-night kiss. While it tries to tell us a woman's value is tied to her sex appeal, God does not say that. He values you because he loves you with an everlasting, perfect love. That perfect love only wants what's best for you. As your Father, he desires to build you up, not tear you down; to make your heart strong, not break it.

The Bible describes your body as a temple: a holy, special, sacred place. It is not supposed to be a place where anyone can come in and take what they want and then go on their merry way. It is supposed to be holy ground. Your body is *imago dei*, which means "made in God's image." It is a creation and reflection of God, and should be treated as such, no matter what the world says.

By encouraging you to protect your body, God is trying to protect the daughter he loves. Most of all, he wants to protect your heart. In 1 Corinthians, Paul explains, "Just because something is technically legal doesn't mean that it's spiritually appropriate. If I went around doing whatever I thought I could get by with, I'd be a slave to my whims" (1 Cor. 6:12, The Message). In other words, God gave you free will—he lets you choose. You can have sex, you can share your body with whomever you choose, you can even use your body as a source to try to get affirmation from men—those are all choices and options for you. But that doesn't mean it will be *beneficial*. The bottom line is: it may hurt you in the end.

Why does your heart tear so badly when these relationships end? Picture an image of a broken heart: a red, fleshy heart, torn down the middle by a jagged seam. When you have sex with someone, you become "one flesh" with that person; the two of you are joined as one (Gen. 2:24; 1 Cor. 6:12–20). Then, when the relationship ends and you go one way while he goes the other—whether after one night or ten years—the flesh of your heart *rips*.

If that happens again and again, you may eventually carry the wounds of those relationships into the relationship with your husband—because sexual sin is one that you actually carry within your body (1 Cor. 6:18). So not only are you bringing your husband a body that has been explored by other men, but also you are bringing him a heart that has been torn again and again. Ultimately, you will regret the choices you made to share your body with others and wish you had saved it for the one with whom you spend your life.

When my husband, Shane, and I dated, we were in our late twenties and didn't know many people who were saving themselves for marriage. To some we might have seemed crazy, but we both had suffered the consequences of our poor choices in the past; now we wanted to do things God's way. We had already learned the hard way that his ways are best. But it was *not easy*!

We were wild about each other and crazy in love. When the lines of sexual purity got blurry and we began to struggle with how far was too far, Shane pulled the line back so far that we were *absolutely sure* we were being pure. After our dates, he would give me a quick kiss good night, then quote the one word from Scripture that saved our relationship: "Flee!" Then he would turn around and go home! It always made us giggle—it still does—but it worked.

"Flee" comes from 1 Corinthians 6:18, that says, "Flee from sexual immorality." That is the best advice I can give you. Flee from exercising your sexuality outside of marriage.

Before you have sex, find someone who believes you are precious enough to first commit to you for life. Hopefully, he will protect you as Shane did with me. He made me feel *worth* waiting for. He made me feel like my value was based on so much more than just my flesh. Can you imagine what a relief that was after my life in the modeling industry?

You deserve that too. You are precious. You are loved by God. That is your affirmation. That is your validation.

Shane and I share a healthy relationship with each other, and we've been blessed with two beautiful children. I don't take these gifts for granted and believe they are a direct result of honoring God with our bodies during our engagement. So it's a choice you make. Ultimately, by choosing to do things God's way in a world that scoffs at his protective boundaries, you will find that his blessings will be *yours*. You will also find your affirmation will never hinge on something as fleeting as your sex appeal—it will come from God, a source that never changes and never stops loving you.

It's in the Word

Here's the good news: Through Eve came three children—Cain, Abel, and Seth. Cain and Abel perished because of jealousy and murder. But through Seth, God promised that a Redeemer would come, One who would remove our shame forever and bring us back to the garden, in communion with him.

That promise was for a Savior. When Jesus came, Hebrews 12:2 says, "For the joy set before him [he] endured the cross, scorning its shame," putting our sins to death once and for all. Even though for a long time I carried shame in my heart, I have realized that we do not need to carry the shame. Jesus *became* our shame so that we could be set free from it.

Jesus came to bind up the brokenhearted; he came to set the captives free. If you are held captive by sexual sin, if you are still carrying its shame or have a jagged, torn heart, give it to him. That's why he came, that's why he died, that's why he rose in new life—to give *us* new life!

My favorite verse says, "Those who look to him are radiant; their faces are *never* covered with shame" (Ps. 34:5, emphasis added). The day I walked down the aisle to marry Shane, I was pure, free, and radiant—not because of what I did, but because of what Jesus did for me. Faith in him removed my shame forever, replacing it with light, hope, and a future.

Do you need a perfect affirmation? Do you need someone to say, "You are special, you are precious, you are beautiful"? Isaiah 43:4 says that since you are precious and dearly loved by God, he will give men in exchange for your life. Namely, he gave his Son—who was beaten, spat upon, whipped, rejected, accused, and, finally, nailed to a cross. It wasn't so that you would be condemned and left in chains, but so that you would be free!

If that is not the ultimate act of love, I don't know what is. That is not a love that wants to *take*, but a love that *gives and gives and gives*. That, my friend, is a love that never runs dry, never walks out, and does not leave you longing. Instead, it fills the longing until it overflows.

Finally, that is a love *that washes and washes and washes* it away until we are completely clean again.

"Everything is *permissible* for me"—but not everything is *beneficial*.
— 1 CORINTHIANS 6:12, EMPHASIS ADDED

So God created man *in his own image*, in the image of God he created him; male and female he created them.
— GENESIS 1:27, EMPHASIS ADDED

Do you not know that *your body is a temple* of the Holy Spirit, who is in you, whom you have received from God? You are not your own; you were bought at a price. Therefore *honor God with your body*.
— 1 CORINTHIANS 6:19–20, EMPHASIS ADDED

"Come now, let us reason together," says the LORD. "Though your sins are like *scarlet*, they shall be as white as *snow*; though they are red as *crimson*, they shall be like *wool*."
— ISAIAH 1:18, EMPHASIS ADDED

Chapter 2

THE PERFECT ACCEPTANCE

Girls, Jealousy, and the Comparison Game

ina sits in her underwear, applying her makeup in the morning light that streams through the window. I'm on the phone with the agency, jotting down appointments: a lingerie casting at nine thirty, a magazine go-see at ten, a request casting at eleven, two more between twelve and two, a commercial audition at two thirty, and three photographers to meet between three and seven.

My booker also reminds me I'm having dinner with Marcello, the recruiter I met in Nina's office the summer after I graduated college. I had plans to go directly to New York to work with Ford Models, but he convinced me it would be better to come to Milan first to do the runway and fill my portfolio with pages from the European magazines— with this, he said, I could make a lot more money in the Big Apple.

Tina gets mascara in her eye and cringes while I lay the map on the table. I chart the route for the day, jotting

*down metro stops, highlighting streets. The doorbell rings.
She drops her wand and rushes to the door. "It must be
Val!" she squeals.*

*Val is five foot seven with light brown skin and brown
hair. She is dressed in out-of-style, cork-healed sandals and
a plain dress. Both from Norway, Val and Tina had lived
and worked together in Greece.*

*Val sleeps on our couch—the agency set it up. We never
have a choice regarding our roommates; the apartments are
a constant revolving door of girls coming from all corners
of the world, having been summoned by the agencies that
promise them work, stardom, and success.*

*Val is too short to do the shows, so she's come to Milan
at a bad time. The city is flooded with models, and castings
are packed with long, lanky, or stunningly curvaceous girls
either straight out of high school or sent from New York.*

*The dynamic in our apartment is dicey: we are all young
and looking for something—this unites us. But at the same
time we are competing with each other—this divides us.*

*As I work in Milan—doing magazines, covers, and now
the runway—I notice that Val seems to grow more and
more bitter, throwing out biting comments beneath feigned
joy. Genuine Tina, on the other hand, seems truly happy for
me. But beneath that is a sense of inadequacy that I have
also felt at times: she makes jokes about her own rejection,
deep down wishing she was the one being picked.*

*Tina and I spend many nights waltzing back and forth
on the wood floor of our apartment, wearing bicycle shorts
and high heels, practicing for the shows. She always reminds
me to keep my elbows in—they have a tendency to jut out
from a childhood accident. And I remind her to keep her left
shoulder down, an imperfection also caused by an injury in
her early years. Tall Tina is pretty but not gorgeous, her face
pleasant but not perfect, her body lean but not sexy. Yet she*

always walks with confidence and poise. She has big, spar-
kling eyes and a round face, but the best thing about her is
her bubbly personality.

In this business, though, personality is a very small piece
of the pie. It's about how we look, period. The agents don't
hesitate to tell me I should straighten my hair, get collagen
injections in my lips, and consider breast implants—none
of which I do.

"They're trying to clone us!" Tina sometimes hollers. "They
want us all to look like Claudia Schiffer!" It's an impossibility
that makes us laugh. But in an odd way, it also hurts. We are
never enough as we are. And for Tina and Val, it seems the
constant attention to their flaws steals the life out of them.

In three months' time Val will be long gone, and another
girl will be sleeping on the couch. Although Tina and Val
enjoy their share of nightclub life in Milan, they do not
muster much work. Bottom line, Val has legs too thick and
short, and skin too temperamental.

Bounce-in-her-step Tina never gets any shows either; her
frame is just not square enough for the meticulous eyes of
the designers—her shoulder plagues her. Over time, I watch
her lose her carefree spirit and disintegrate into a depressed,
rejected, homesick girl, always complaining that her head
pounds and stomach aches.

What We're Really Longing For

Acceptance: *to be received favorably; to be*
approved of; to be endured without protest

We are born wanting to be accepted as we are. We are not
born comparing ourselves to others. But somewhere along
the line, we begin to mark our value along the scale of what
other women look like or how they perform.

We continually ask, "Where do I fall on the beauty scale? Where do I fall on the success scale?"

Unfortunately, the answer to those questions, in our world, brings us to "the acceptance factor." In this generation, beauty equals acceptance, and if beauty doesn't bring it, performance will.

The deep longing we have to be accepted as we are leads us into an unhealthy comparison game with other women. We ultimately want to be chosen *over* the other girl while at the same time not be rejected by her. We want to rank higher on the acceptance scale. When we find ourselves *not* being accepted—as Tina and Val, and later I, did—we internalize the feeling that we ended up at the bottom of the scale, and that *bites*.

I left the apartment without eating because the first casting was for lingerie. As the photographer flipped through my portfolio, I hoped he would look into my eyes, but he didn't. He just handed me a white lace bra and panties and pointed me toward the changing room. I tried them on, and they videotaped me from all sides while I tried to pretend it wasn't shockingly embarrassing.

I didn't have any fat left on my body—I didn't have anything to fill the bra either. I was sure my inadequacy was written all over my face. As I changed back into my clothes, I was so annoyed with the agency. They knew I was not a lingerie model! Why did they send me on stuff like this?

As I walked past the line of girls waiting their turn, it occurred to me that *every one of them* would try on the same bra and panties that I just did; I was glad I had arrived early, but now I wanted a shower!

I took the metro to the outskirts of town and hiked several blocks, while the straps of the new shoes Mom and I had bought for Italy sliced into the tendon on the back of my ankle. Several girls ran past me as it began to rain, worrying about their hair and makeup. I hid under the giant black hood of my raincoat.

I arrived at my next appointment. A lady from the magazine—the one considering me for their beauty segment—asked me to stand by the window so she could see my skin in the light, so I did.

"Typical," she muttered after only glancing at my face. She snapped my portfolio closed and handed it back to me.

Clenching my teeth, I forced a smile, shook her hand, and walked out.

"I am *not* typical!" I yelled in the elevator on the way down.

I took the metro four stops east, changed twice, got off, and walked seven blocks on huge cobblestones to get to the next appointment. The shoe straps continued to dig into my nerves the whole way.

The photographer was so captivated with the fourteen-year-old untouched beauty sitting in front of him that he put his hand up for me to wait. Her mother was with her—it was the one and only time I ever saw *that* in Europe.

The girl was wearing a schoolgirl's uniform and a pair of tennies. She had a look on her face that told me she hadn't yet been duped by the world.

"I was her once," I said to myself. At twenty-one—an age that some people in this business consider to be older—I was smarter; I had been around the world and back a few times. That didn't change the fact, however, that I was as prone to jealousy as the next girl.

As I waited, I was suddenly envious of her clean bare face, tennis shoes, and simplicity. I felt awkward in my own made-up face, my new heels, and the body I had worked so hard to sculpt. When my turn came about, the photographer was still so enraptured with her that he flipped through my portfolio, gave me only half a glance, and sent me away.

At the next casting I waited more than an hour to try on a little black dress and pretend like I was shaving my legs for the camera. Every girl there was checking out the legs of the other girls, summing up on a scale of 1 to 10 how she looked in the dress. For some reason it made me feel better when I saw the cottage cheese on the back of one girl's thighs, but worse when another had cleavage spilling from the neckline.

After a few more metro changes and some confusion reading the street map, I arrived at the mirrored building that houses L'Oréal. There I discovered they "liked me a lot" but wanted someone with straight hair that can go curly, not curly hair that can go straight.

As I left, I wondered again why the agency even sent me there, and I saw a girl with silky-straight, shiny hair swishing down her back going in after me. "*Hmmph*, this one's for her," I thought.

I ducked into a café to get a double espresso and called the agency. "Where have you been?" they screamed at me. "We've been trying to find you! You have an appointment at Armani! They are waiting for you! Go! Now!"

Armani? Since I first came to Milan, my agency had targeted me as their type. I wanted to work at Armani more than I wanted *anything*. I immediately broke out in a sweat.

Suddenly my feet didn't hurt. I raced to the metro, fought the madness of three line changes, and within an hour I was walking down *Via Borgonuovo*, the street on which Armani built his empire. The show season had not officially started yet, but this call was for a small preseason show.

The cobblestones on *Via Borgonuovo* shimmered from recent rain; the afternoon sun lit them up like pure gold. Clicking my heels down the side of the street, I looked up. The towering buildings were adorned by exquisite angels and snarling gargoyles carved into the façades.

I stopped in front of number 26. The door was so massive it made me feel like Dorothy at the gates of Oz. "When you walk in the door, act like, 'I'm exactly what you want,'" a seasoned model once told me. So I straightened my skirt, rolled my shoulders back, and jiggled the giant brass knocker.

The door clicked open. An imposing guard offered me a seat. I sat down and waited, crossing and recrossing my legs, while sweat threatened to stick them together.

A man with jet-black hair and pale skin walked in and introduced himself as Matteo. He led me down a hallway where we met a tall man in a tapered suit. Matteo told me to walk for him. So I did.

Walking down the hall in fluid strides, I reached the end and turned—just as my show booker had taught me, just as Tina and I had practiced. First I turned my head, locking my eyes, then my body followed, and I strutted back with my hips and shoulders fastened. Matteo nodded in approval; the tall man said something in Italian and strode off, his large, imposing frame disappearing down the hallway.

Next I met a stern woman with bronze freckles, who quickly leafed through my portfolio while glancing at me in quick flashes. She stopped at one of my pictures and made a phone call.

Matteo came back in and told me to walk down the street to number 21. Back on the glistening cobblestones, I wondered if I would actually meet the man at the throne of this kingdom.

Inside the massive, ornate building, a big bald guy, who looked like a bodyguard, motioned for me to follow him. He led me down spiral stairs to an auditorium and left me standing amid its top rows.

Intimidation rushed over me like a wave. The enormous room reminded me of an ice-skating stadium. Rows of seats circled the oval palace, culminating in a runway at the center. I took a few steps down and saw people sitting in chairs, looking up at three models wearing netted berets and flared skirts on the runway. The girls swiveled at the base of the "T" while stylists knelt in front of them, pinning and primping their skirts.

Comparisons fuel jealousy; jealousy fuels hatred; hatred fuels anger; and anger, in turn, fuels fear.

When I got to the main floor, a woman escorted me backstage into the largest, most cavernous dressing room I have ever seen. It was lined with rows and rows of clothing racks, each tagged with names and numbers. Models wearing nude G-string underwear stood next to the racks as stylists help them change.

Matteo appeared. I was so nervous I asked if I could pee, but he shook his head no.

Then Giorgio walked in. He was medium height, leathery tan, and trim. His whitish-silver hair contrasted strikingly with his suntanned skin and penetrating eyes. He walked up to me, shook my hand, and looked directly into my eyes: I felt like I was plugged into an electric socket. He put his hands around my waist and I could feel his fingers pressing into the space below my ribs. Matteo handed him my book.

He flipped through it, nodded, and walked away. A stylist took me to a dressing rack and had me put on a lavender chiffon dress that fell over me like a breeze. I was terrified that they would put me in super-high heels. I took off my small bandages while I waited, hoping the shoes wouldn't show the open blisters on my heels and toes.

Then, without any warning—or even any shoes—Armani came up beside me, took me by the hand, and gave me a little shove: "Walk!"

Taken off guard, I stumbled forward, my head and torso leading the way instead of my hips. When I turned, I completely forgot to do it right—I turned my body first and my head last, wobbling. I walked back to him as best I could, feeling as awkward as a little girl trying on her mother's big-girl clothes.

He uttered, "*Tch*," and with a little wave of his hand, dismissed me. The blood drained out of my face.

The other models looked at me in pity as I walked off the stage. The stylist escorted me back to the dressing room, hung up the dress, and walked away. I stood there, naked, clasping my arms over my breasts, hoping that she would come back and give me another outfit to wear.

Looking around the room, I noticed a girl with long blonde hair like mine. She was bent over, putting on stockings; the bones of her spine protruded from her back like a row of knuckles. I suddenly realized she was my neighbor and wondered if she ever ate anything—she was *so* thin.

Shivering and embarrassed, I felt like my feet were glued to the carpet; I could not move. My stomach was hot and clenched tight as a fist. Finally Matteo caught my eye from across the room and sent someone over to tell me to get dressed in my own clothes. I did, and then he came over.

"He likes you," he said, "but not for the shows. Maybe for the print."

I sighed.

"There will be other times," he said. "Thank you for your time. Now, do you remember the way out?"

I nodded.

"*Ciao*," he said, kissing me on both cheeks. Then he turned his back and started talking to another girl.

Outside, on *Via Borgonuovo*, I gave in to the pain in my feet. "I blew it, I blew it," I muttered to myself. "I got to Armani and I blew it." Tears welled up in my eyes, blurring the street before me, and I nearly twisted my ankle on the cobblestones.

"I am such an idiot," I whispered. I hated myself for being so stupid. I hated myself for stumbling. Tears spilled down my cheeks.

At the end of the street, there was a stone stump. I sat down on it, let my shoulders slump around my chest, and cried softly into my hands.

After a few moments, I felt a tap on my shoulder. Looking up, I saw an old man with silver hair and big blue eyes, leaning on a cane.

"*Perchè lei piange ragazza?*" he asked.

Surprised that this man approached me, I told him that I didn't speak Italian. He wanted to know if I spoke French, but I didn't. He seemed disappointed that he couldn't communicate with me.

Shaking his head helplessly, he said, "*Signorina, non piangere. La vita è bella!*"

"I don't understand you," I replied, while tears streamed down my face.

His eyes begged me to understand. "*La vita è bella!*" he exclaimed, waving his arms in the air, motioning to the tree behind him and the sky. "Life…is…byoo-ti-full."

"Life is beautiful. Life is beautiful," he repeated in broken English. Wiping away the tears, I nodded at him. Assured that I understood, he hobbled away, his cane tapping on the troublesome cobblestones.

FROM MY WORLD TO YOURS

Life *is* beautiful. But why do we feel so strongly that it has to do with *us* being beautiful, *us* being accepted?

It's funny to me that people think models have a higher self-esteem than other girls because they have been stamped as beautiful or even attractive. For me, modeling was a constant reminder of where I fell short. I could never be thin enough, and then I was too thin. I could never be successful enough, and then when I was, I had to do more. I was pale when they wanted tan; tall when they wanted small; blonde when they wanted brunette; curvy when they wanted raillike; then raillike when they wanted curvy. And my problem with clumsiness was *never* "in"!

The jealousy, competition, and comparisons between the girls created a never-ending, exhausting cycle, and we *all* came up lacking for the toll it took on us.

When I saw my neighbor dressing backstage at Armani, her long blonde locks spilling over her bony shoulders, the perfect form of every vertebra outlining her back, I was jealous that she was picked and I wasn't.

Several weeks later, Armani had the call for his real "big" shows of the season, and surprisingly, I got another chance to walk for him. The second time around I did *not* blow it. I walked with confidence, and from among thousands competing, I was picked, along with about thirty other girls, to do both the *Emporio* and the *Giorgio* shows—so of course I was ecstatic!

But this time, my neighbor from across the hall wasn't picked.

The eyes of God are the eyes of acceptance despite our imperfections, despite the shortcomings, despite the mistakes. The eyes of God are the eyes of grace.

After the *Emporio*, I came home to find her sobbing on the landing outside our apartments. I asked her what was wrong, and through bloodshot eyes she told me she had come to Milan specifically for the shows but didn't get any. I tried to console her, telling her that at least she got the preseason show—for which I had been rejected—so she should at least be happy about that. But she just turned her back, went inside, and slammed the door, angry at having fallen to the bottom— or for her, *below the bottom*—of the scale.

To my own surprise, I wasn't nearly as happy as I thought I would be when I finally did do Armani's shows, partly because I felt internally plagued by the other girls' suffering over their rejection. Hey, I wanted acceptance too—not just from Armani and the clients, but from the girls as well. There was this unsettling feeling hanging over our apartment as if I had "made out" while the girls around me unjustly didn't.

———

Rejection is a huge part of the modeling business—rejection I was used to. But the comparison game was more subtle. It was an accusing voice inside of me that asked, "What does she have that you don't?"

The first time I really began to ask that question, I was fifteen years old and up for a national commercial for Pop-Tarts. Mom and I drove from San Diego to Los Angeles five times for callbacks.

Finally, the client narrowed it down from hundreds of girls to only one other girl and me. All my friends and family, and their friends and family, were so excited I was about to be on television; you would have thought I was going to be elected governor. So when at the final hour they chose the other girl, I felt like I let everyone down.

Every time I saw that commercial, I was furious. I kept asking myself, "What does she have that I don't have? Does she smile better, dance better, eat Pop-Tarts better, or schmooze better?"

Well, for one thing, she had freckles. She was cute. She was like a young Drew Barrymore. I was more like a young Daryl Hannah. I didn't have freckles; I was tall and reedy, not "cute." Maybe that's what it was. Who knows?

In Hamburg, Germany, where I lived for my first summer after high school graduation, my Danish roommate was the Pop-Tarts girl revived. She looked just like the girl who years earlier had stolen that job from me. And guess what? I seemed to steal every job away from her that summer. She had freckles; she was shorter; she was cuter. I was taller, more sophisticated looking, I guess, and it seemed as though every job we both interviewed for, I got.

I knew it had nothing to do with *her* or *me*; it was *always* about what *they*—*the clients*—wanted. We were *mannequins!* In fact, that is the French word for model: *le mannequin*. In other words, we were being bought and sold based on appearance, and it wasn't our fault if we weren't what they wanted.

But my Danish roommate did not see it that way. She saw me all made up when I came home from jobs, and instantly comparison led to jealousy, and jealousy to hatred. She would just turn her back and shut her door. I had a much better relationship with our other roommate, who was a tall, big-boned brunette—we looked nothing alike and made great friends.

Again, this doesn't just go on in the modeling industry. This is the dynamic every female experiences at one time or another—and for some girls, at all times.

⁓

A model's portfolio is her book of worth. At castings we would exchange books just for a look-see. The summer after my freshman year of college, I was eighteen and lived in Paris. The models' apartment I lived in, right off the famous *Champs-Élysées*, was a classic example of the comparison game.

One of my roommates was a *Vogue* cover model in her mid-twenties. Lying on the floor of our apartment, I flipped through her portfolio. Her Greek-bronzed skin, big lips, voluptuous figure, and bare bust caked in sand and sweat made me feel like an insignificant little girl in the presence of what the world celebrates as real, live womanhood.

Back then I had nothing in my portfolio to compare to her face and body splashed over the pages of *Elle*.

My other roommate in Paris was a Calvin Klein model from Spain. Victoria had been traveling the world since she was fourteen. She knew how to speak French, how to navigate the city, where the best bars and bistros were, how to get the best drugs, and her book was filled with artwork by renowned photographers. Next to Victoria, I was a nothing, and she made sure I knew it.

"I have been around this business more times than you can count, *Jenni-fur*," she would say, taking a long drag off her hand-rolled cigarette. "Believe me, you know nothing!"

The one roommate I did hold a candle to was a young Czech girl who came to town with hardly anything in her portfolio. Compared to her, I knew a lot. And if you held my pictures up to hers, mine won.

Comparisons, comparisons, comparisons, comparisons. I could not escape them; even when I didn't *want* to be compared, even when I was content with being myself, when I felt like our differences truly made us unique and weren't a cause for jealousy, still, the comparisons were there. We all used each other as measuring sticks of our worth.

Comparisons fuel jealousy; jealousy fuels hatred; hatred fuels anger; and anger, in turn, fuels fear.

When I was in seventh grade, an eighth-grader at my school decided she wanted to kick my you-know-what. She was big, strong, and imposing, and I was toast if she decided to go through with it.

She had also just threatened another blonde-haired, fair-skinned girl at school by holding a razor blade to her face. Pathetic as it may sound right now, at the time, I ended up paying her off in installments from my allowance to ensure my life—and my face—stayed intact. Hey, what can I say? I made a deal. It was self-preservation, mixed with shame and fear.

I guess she had decided, "We *hate Barbie*! So let's kill Barbie." That other blonde girl and I must have been the closest thing to Barbie in her eyes. We were scared to death of that girl. But the truth is, something about *us* made *her* feel *less than*. To make up for it she lashed out. The world we live in said she was less than—lower grades, lower income, didn't fit the Barbie image, so she was mad. And it seemed easiest to be mad at us. I didn't understand it at the time; now I do.

Too bad it took me paying her off for us to form any kind of bond. The bond was: she had proven seniority over me. She was the alpha dog. And as long as I knew my place, there wouldn't be any fangs.

In high school, I had good friends, but I also had a group of girls who hated me. It was as if they were just waiting to see me mess up, and when I did, boy, did they broadcast it. My fall was fodder for their gossip, and they made sure I paid the price for my mistakes.

"You can't be too perfect, or we'll hate you. On the other hand, if you aren't perfect enough, we'll nail you to the wall." Girls can be catty. They can be cruel. The sad thing is, girls know more than anyone how badly we all just want to be accepted. Even though I had nothing in common with that eighth-grade girl at school, and I had no idea how to warm her to me, deep down I just wanted her acceptance.

But true acceptance does not stem from comparisons. True acceptance comes from looking elsewhere for our value—not from using other girls as measuring sticks of our worth.

IT'S IN THE WORD

When Jesus was alive, the Pharisees and teachers of Jewish law—the people who claimed to be the most religious—were actually the people who hated Jesus and finally had him killed. There were a lot of reasons for this, but namely, their comparisons led to jealousy, then to hatred, anger, and finally fear. Jesus was just too *perfect* for them.

For one thing, he called God in heaven his own Father. That really bugged the Pharisees because Jesus seemed a little *too* confident. When they compared themselves to him, they fell short, so they were jealous. On top of it all, Jesus was sinless—he was the only man to ever walk the earth who didn't sin. Obviously, from a human standpoint, this is impossible. But he was the Spirit of God cloaked in flesh. He was perfect.

This is why comparisons fueled jealousy, which led to hatred, and finally, fear. They tried to trick Jesus and trap him, but they couldn't. So they rejected him, beat him, spat on him, and finally murdered him. Simply put, they were afraid of that which they didn't understand. They were afraid of perfect: his perfect love, his perfect relationship with God. His perfect sacrifice terrified them, even unto his last breath.

So people will also hate you if you seem perfect, because it scares them. It is threatening to them. It makes them feel *less than*. And they are just waiting for you to mess up so they can announce to the world that you're *not* perfect—which, of course, none of us are.

When the teachers of the Law and the Pharisees brought the woman who was caught in adultery to the center of their town to stone her, Jesus had a few choice words for them: "If any one of you is without sin, let him be the first to throw a stone at her" (John 8:7). According to the Book of John, they began to slowly walk away, the older ones first, probably because they were more aware of the ways they fell short.

When they were all gone, Jesus stood with her: the one who was without sin with the woman plagued by it. Did he throw a stone at her? No. He could have. He could have judged her. But instead he asked her if anyone was condemning her. She replied that no one was. "Then neither do I," Jesus declared. "Go now and leave your life of sin." (This is my paraphrase of John 8:9–11.)

Oh, the grace. The grace with which he sees us!

The hypocrites pointed their fingers at the woman caught in adultery because that took the focus off themselves. Let's find the girl who messes up and make it public—so everyone will look at *her* and not us.

This is exactly what many girls in high school do, and unfortunately, many grown women do too. They hate you if you are perfect, but they also hate you if you're not. Let's throw stones at the girl who messes up. Let's declare to the world, "Aha! We've caught her red-handed! She's not perfect!"

And Jesus says, "Uh-huh, and what about you? Are you somehow without sin?"

The funny thing is, the Pharisees brought the woman caught in adultery to Jesus as a trap for *him*, "in order to have a basis for accusing him" (John 8:6). And *they* were the accusers. Do you know who the Bible says is the accuser? Satan (Rev. 12:10). Satan accuses God's children all day long.

Isn't it interesting that he worked at this time through "religious" people—accusing, condemning, and pointing the finger, with stone in hand?

Jesus never retaliated when they accused, challenged, and ultimately crucified him because his need for acceptance didn't stem from them! He didn't look to them for acceptance; he looked to the Father. His natural human longing to be accepted was completely fulfilled in his relationship with God.

But if anyone knew what it was to be rejected, it was Jesus Christ.

> He was despised and rejected by men, a man of sorrows, and familiar with suffering. Like one from whom men hide their faces he was despised, and we esteemed him not.
>
> —ISAIAH 53:3

And yet he took our sins and carried our sorrows.

> God has piled all our sins, everything we've done wrong, on him, on him. He was beaten, he was tortured, but he didn't say a word. Like a lamb taken to be slaughtered and like a sheep being sheared, he took it all in silence. Justice miscarried, and he was led off—and did anyone really know what was happening? He died without a thought for his own welfare, beaten bloody for the sins of my people....Even though he'd never hurt a soul or said one word that wasn't true....The plan was that he give himself as an offering for sin so that he'd see life come from it—life, life, and more life.
>
> —ISAIAH 53:6–10, THE MESSAGE

Jesus bore the woman's sins. He even bore the sins of the Pharisees, the hypocrites. He bore your sin and mine. Suddenly we all don't seem so different anymore, do we? Suddenly we realize that we all "fall short" of perfect (Rom. 3:23).

When Jesus looked at the woman caught in adultery, he saw her through compassionate eyes. He saw her as he sees all of us: fallen and in need of rescue; broken and in need of repair; rejected and in need of acceptance...in need of his grace.

The eyes of God are the eyes of acceptance despite your imperfections, despite your shortcomings, despite your mistakes. The eyes of God are the eyes of grace. As a girl who follows God, or at least searches for him, you must take on eyes of grace. If he—being perfect in every way—looks at imperfect people with eyes of acceptance, shouldn't you and I begin to look at others this way too? If he isn't going to condemn, who are we to judge?

If he who was without sin is not going to throw a stone at us, maybe we need to drop our rocks.

Are you in need of perfect acceptance? I'm sorry to say that people won't always give that to you. When your need for acceptance is fulfilled only through imperfect people, you will always find yourself wanting. And when your value is based on the comparison scale, you will always find yourself unsatisfied.

God, who made you, knows that at the very core of your heart you just want to be accepted as you are. But he also knows that what you are longing for can't be filled by what the world has to offer. When Jesus went to the cross for us, in essence, he said, "I ACCEPT YOU!" in neon lights, with letters written in his own blood and tears. He said, "I don't want your sins to separate you from a holy God anymore. Everyone falls short of perfect; all stumble. I want you to be free from comparisons. I want you to be free to be the girl God made."

Psalm 139 says he made us each individually, with unique bodies, talents, gifts, and plans for our lives. The differences between us are purposeful—they *do not* make some of us "more than" and some of us "less than." When you see other people through the eyes of the cross, suddenly, at the core, we are all the same. Yet from the center of that core to the wrapping of our flesh, we are all unique; we are different.

When we look at each other through eyes of grace, those differences become beautiful expressions of God's handprint on Earth. Tina's lopsided shoulder and my elbows make us individuals with stories to tell. Truly beautiful women are those who can accept and celebrate our uniqueness—both in the flesh part of us and the inner parts that no one can see.

As one who was once plagued by comparisons, today, this is how I feel: I am not afraid of the qualities you have that make you appear more brilliant or beautiful. I am grateful for what you have been given, and I hope you will use those gifts to bring more grace to the world around you.

Oh, and if you mess up, I'm here when you fall. I will lend a hand; I will not throw a stone. Because I am just like you.

For you created my inmost being; *you knit me together* in my mother's womb. I praise you because I am fearfully and wonderfully made; your works are wonderful, I know that full well.

—PSALM 139:13–14, EMPHASIS ADDED

There is *no difference*, for *all* have sinned and *fall short* of the glory of God, and are justified freely by his grace through the redemption that came by Christ Jesus.

—ROMANS 3:22–24, EMPHASIS ADDED

We all stumble in many ways. If anyone is *never* at fault in what he says, he is a *perfect* man.

—JAMES 3:2, EMPHASIS ADDED

Do not judge, and you will not be judged. *Do not condemn*, and you will not be condemned. *Forgive*, and you will be forgiven.

—LUKE 6:37, EMPHASIS ADDED

Chapter 3

THE PERFECT IMAGE

Getting Real

I am nervously walking the quiet catacombs of the Parisian underground. The long, dark hallways where people rush during the day are chillingly cold and silent at night. I have never been down here alone in the dark. It is well past midnight, after a concert, and Victoria and my other roommates stayed on the train to go to an all-night rave. But I have to work tomorrow; I have a five-day trip to Sweden. I have to change lines and get home.

Barely able to see through the shadows, I walk across the platform to get to my next train, looking over my shoulder every few seconds to make sure no one comes up behind me. I feel helpless; if someone wanted to, he could shove me onto the tracks.

When the train finally comes, I sit in a window seat. Leaning my head against the glass, I notice my reflection. My skin is opalescent and hair falls in ivory ribbons, but eyes are red as a burn.

The train starts moving with a jerk. My attention dives into the flashing darkness: a fleeting array of metal and concrete and lightlessness. And when the headlights of a passing train illuminate the window, all I can see is the blackness through which I travel...and the empty, drunken expression of a man whose body jiggles with the rhythm of the train.

The train only goes three stops then shuts down. Confused, I follow the other passengers onto the landing and ask a man what's happening. He makes a slicing action across his throat and points to his watch. It is 3:00 a.m.

I follow the crowd up the stairs, right into the red-light district of Paris—a place I have never seen. The people from the metro disperse, and I hesitantly walk down the sidewalk. Nude women slither behind neon-lit windows, groping themselves. Winos and prostitutes litter the sidewalk; a pimp approaches me speaking in a French drawl. I step back into the street in hopes of hailing a cab, but realize I have no cash left on me—only a metro pass, which is useless at this point.

Panicking, I see some people boarding a bus, so I bolt for it, but the bus pulls away and I can see the faces of the passengers staring blankly at me from behind the glass. I run alongside the bus, screaming, "Let me on!" until a man stands up and yells at the driver to stop, which he does. The doors swing open, I jump aboard; the man walks forward and pays my fare.

My heart racing, I profusely thank the man who helped me and show him my sweaty, crumpled metro map, pointing to where I need to go. He nods. The other passengers stare at me judgmentally, as if I am a hooker just getting off work. Refusing to ingest their glares, I hold my head up as the bus winds through the dark, wet street.

Finally the man nudges me and I get off, following some people who hurry down a flight of stairs back into the metro. I run with them onto the landing and jump on a train just as its doors close. After a few stops I show my map to someone, pointing to my destination. "Non! Non!"

he exclaims, telling me I am going the wrong way. I could cry.

At the next stop I get off the train, jog up the stairs, cross the bridge, then walk down a dark stairwell, where I practically bump into a man crouched on the stairs. He is groaning, and when I lean in closer to see if he is hurt, I realize he is masturbating! Horrified, I race to the platform just as a train slams its doors shut and pulls away.

My heart practically stops in my throat as I realize the danger I'm in. There is no train in sight, and there won't be for who knows how long. Now I see three drunk guys laughing and fooling around at the end of the landing, and here I am—tall, blonde, eighteen, alone, scared . . . and stupid. I stand frozen against the wall, praying that no one will hurt me.

A homeless man with a dirty brown face stumbles around the corner. He begins to stammer at me in French, gesturing wildly, spit spraying from his mouth. I tell him to leave me alone, but he keeps approaching closer and closer. Out of the corner of my eye I see the three drunk guys jeering him on. He waves his whiskey bottle around as he gets more and more vehement that I respond to whatever he is saying.

"Please leave me alone," I beg, looking around for help. But there is none. The drunk guys are getting closer and closer now, whistling and calling to me. The homeless man starts laughing, his corroded teeth making him look like a wild dog.

I am terrified.

Then I hear a rumble from the tracks. A train is coming. I just pray it's on my side of the landing. The light from the train blazes out of the tunnel. It's my train! I run to get on.

The three drunk guys follow me into the car but sit a few rows away. They keep blowing me kisses, laughing, and motioning for me to sit on their laps; I pretend to ignore them.

At the next stop, I jump up and run out of the car, race down the platform, and board another car. Utterly relieved, I sit across from an elderly woman wearing thick nylon stockings and rubber-soled shoes.

Immediately, I can feel her looks of shame boring into my legs. I'm wearing brown leather sandals and a jean jacket over a flimsy tie-dyed dress that stops just short of my knees. The occasional flashes of light through the train windows light up the little white hairs on my thighs. I am dressed like a California girl, but now I realize that, since I have been in Paris, I have never seen a French woman wearing a miniskirt without stockings. With my teased hair, stoned eyes, and bare legs, I realize I am the epitome of the classless American; she probably thinks I'm a whore.

Without warning, the train stops and the lights go out. I ask the woman what's wrong and she points to the stairs and walks off. When I get to the top of the stairwell I have no idea where I am, so I show my torn metro map to a man who looks kind, begging him with my eyes to show me the way. He points me in the direction toward home.

The man follows me from a distance for at least an hour. I speed walk while whispering, "Please don't let him hurt me, please don't let him hurt me." I keep picturing the man throwing me into the shadows of the bushes, raping and choking me to death in the corners of the parks that line the road. But he turns the other way once I am on the great, wide boulevard, the Champs-Élysées.

The Arc de Triomphe *is in sight, the enormous ivory structure framing the city, telling me I am near my apartment. The sky fades from navy to white; a bright light comes over the city. I turn onto the* Rue de Grenelle, *my street, and come to the gate of my apartment building. It's locked. I live across from the agency "so they can keep an eye on us," but it isn't open yet. I go down an alley and head to the back gate.*

In front of the wrought-iron bars stands a saddled white horse. I can hardly believe what I'm seeing. What is a horse doing tied up on my gate in the middle of the night? It seems like something from a dream. I look around for an owner, but see no one. Finally I just pet the horse, kiss it, and open the gate. The dew-covered grass brushes my ankles as I cross the courtyard to my front door.

I go inside and take a long, hot shower. Streams of water rush over my goose-pimpled skin as I silently say thank you.

In a daze, I pack my bags and dress for the day. By the time the sun peaks its head over the city, I am heading back down to the subway to catch a train to Sweden.

What We're Really Longing For

Image: *an imitation of a person or thing; a representation, likeness, impression or conception of oneself; an illusion*

When the pictures come out from that Swedish editorial and plaster themselves all over the shop windows of Paris, I am on the cover of the magazine, smiling, cuddled up nice and warm in a winter sweater. I look happy, safe, secure, and comfortable. I do not look alone, lost, confused, or terrified. I do not look the way I had felt the night before.

With the work of the makeup artist, the lighting, the clothes, and my expertise in wearing "the mask," no one could have ever guessed about my escapades that lasted until dawn. No one could know that my heart was still slowing down from my race through the dark.

An image is an imitation of a person, a representation, a likeness, an illusion. Sometimes we must dispel the illusion that what we see in magazines is true to life.

At fourteen years old, my roommate Victoria landed a million-dollar contract with Calvin Klein. She was truly a Spanish beauty: almond eyes; olive skin; sassy, pursed lips; and long chestnut hair. She had a figure like one would imagine Eve's to be: a narrow waist, wide hips, and fleshy arms that jiggled as she raised them high over the crowds in the nightclubs.

I met Victoria in the agency the first day I arrived in Paris. When the owner of the agency asked her to show me around the city for a day of castings, Victoria looked at my cheap American sundress and sandals and crinkled up her freckled nose. At eighteen, after modeling internationally for six years, she had no interest in showing some newcomer the ropes. But she relented, and I was glad. To be honest, without her, I don't think I would have survived Paris. She became my roommate, guide, friend, teacher, and protector.

One morning we were walking down the *Champs-Élysées* on our way to the metro. People bustled along the sidewalks while cars traveled bumper to bumper through the *Arc de Triomphe*. The sidewalk cafés streamed with people who lined up for caffé lattes and croissants to go. Both of us were dolled up for a day of castings, and I walked beside her as she navigated the way to the metro.

As we shuffled through the crowd, I suddenly felt someone reach up my miniskirt and grab me right between the legs. Gasping for breath, I stopped and looked around me. Below me on the sidewalk was a bum dressed in rags, gripping a bottle of gin in one hand and my underwear with the other.

"You pig! You disgusting pig!" I screamed, kicking at him. Victoria, who had walked on unknowingly, turned and saw what was happening. Pushing people aside, she ran back and pulled me away from him. Yelling, I told her what he had done, and she ran up to him, cursing at him in French and spitting on him. I tried to go after him again; I wanted to kick the bottle out of his hand and smash it in his face, but she pulled me back, yanking me by my hair down the street.

"I can't believe this!" I screamed. "Get the police!"

But she wouldn't let me go back for revenge. "That kind is dangerous. You don't know what he'll do. He could throw that bottle in your face and cut you up!"

"But, but…" was all I could reply.

She dug her fingers into my arm and led me through the crowd. A tear streamed down my face. "Get a hold of yourself," she said to me, her voice hard as stone. "Forget about it." I smoothed my skirt and straightened my shoulders, glancing back once more before we stepped into the underground.

That happened in the morning. For the rest of the day, we hiked up and down the streets on buses and metros; met with photographers, clients, and magazine editors; tried on bathing suits, fur coats, and suits; and smiled for the camera as we vied for jobs. And I did what Victoria said. I "forgot" about it. I buried it, the same way I buried the fear of being young and alone in a scary world. That was just the way modeling was for me—stuffing the real emotions of the real girl in search of maintaining a perfect image.

Victoria and I became as good of friends as two models can be, considering one came from one end of the spectrum and the other from the other end; one on her way some place, the other going somewhere else; one climbing the ladder of fashion, the other desperately grabbing at the rungs as she fell.

As her roommate, I learned a lot about Victoria. I learned about the *real* girl beneath the image of Calvin Klein, behind the riding boots and starched white shirts. Underneath the image of that young girl looking innocently into the camera was a woman lost and running too. Desperate for affection and acceptance, Victoria was as tainted a person as you can find. She trusted no one; she had been, in her own words, "screwed too many times."

Having been on her own since she was fourteen, Victoria essentially had no one. Her parents—both models who became famous in the '60s—had been jet-setting around the world and cheating on each other for as long as she could remember.

As a teen, she had their summer villa on the beach to herself for months on end. There she had wild parties with more drugs and naked people than she could even recall. She loved to boast about a time, at fifteen, when she "lived on acid," hallucinating on modeling jobs, fooling photographers, boyfriends, agents, and, for that matter, the world. It was the world that she duped more than anyone. In ads, she was the image of self-assured beauty personified. Talk about an illusion.

Curled up like a lioness on the floor of our Parisian apartment, Victoria heckled about the fact that she had spent *every single cent* of her million-dollar paycheck. She owed money to several agencies, which was why she was in Paris now, to pay off her debt. The problem for Victoria was that she didn't look like that fourteen-year-old girl anymore. Her body had developed curves where there were none before, and the innocence was long gone from her eyes.

In front of photographers, she was the epitome of confidence, wily seduction, and almost snobbish pride. But at home, she hated her reflection in the mirror, worried endlessly about being fat, smoked constantly, did drugs, and alternated between starving herself and bingeing. Victoria was as insecure and afraid in the world as I was.

Each night, she rolled hash cigarettes, drank wine, lounged on the floor, and told stories about the business, about how much she knew and how much she had seen, reminding me constantly of how little I knew. At the time I was intrigued, sometimes dumbfounded but nevertheless impressed. Today, as I imagine her hazel eyes looking at me, I can see in them not all that she had gained, but all that she had lost. She had the soul of a very old, tired woman who had lived a long and unsatisfying life, the soul of someone who had seen too many goodbyes and too many losses.

 The world is much more interested in image than it is in reality. It wants to believe that the girl in the picture is as satisfied as she looks.

But if she ever caught me looking at her closely, she would just crack a joke about how American I was, how naïve I was, suck hard on her joint, and launch into yet another story about another photographer, another party, another stint on drugs, and another blank and stolen piece of her memory.

FROM MY WORLD TO YOURS

The world is much more interested in image than it is in reality. It wants to believe that the girl in the picture is as satisfied as she looks. The world doesn't *really* want to know that the girl in the picture is no longer the girl in the picture—she has lost her innocence, her faith in people, her money, her hope, and her security.

I don't think the world really cares that the girl in the picture essentially feels abandoned by her parents in search of money and fame. I also don't think the world really wants to know that the girl on the magazine poster in the store window was just attacked by a bum in the street or followed by a faceless man in the night. The world feels better thinking the girl in the picture is as happy and secure as she looks.

Unfortunately, the world treats the girl in the picture as if she is as disposable as the paper the magazine ad is printed on. Certainly Calvin Klein, by the time I'd met Victoria, had moved on to another teenage girl. And her untouched beauty would soon become tainted too. But I believe it's my job to tell you about the girl in the picture, because I was the girl in the picture and I lived with girls in the pictures.

Behind that Calvin Klein ad, behind those freckled cheeks and searching eyes, was the real Victoria—the Victoria I knew. I knew her hunger and her thirst; I saw it firsthand. When I left Paris in search of work in Greece, Victoria was still without work, still without family, still in debt, still smoking hash every night, and still dancing in the clubs until four in the morning.

Only eighteen years old and alone in the world, she was still trying to resurrect a modeling career while sleeping with a photographer she had recently met. She was dieting, hating her figure, chain-smoking, drinking, avoiding the gym, and loathing the fact that she couldn't indulge in the cappuccinos, croissants, pasta, and wine that she loved. Victoria was still in fear that she would be rejected for not having the figure she had at fourteen. But most of all, she was still clinging to what she believed was her identity: she was a Calvin Klein model, period.

But that was not a lasting identity. That was only an image, a snapshot, a moment in time, and it was gone. Beneath the image, she had no idea who she was or what her value could be. So I believe she wore a hard mask. She put on a tough façade as a way to protect herself from a world that had promised to make all her dreams come true but failed at every turn. The mask kept her from being real, because if she was real, she would crumble. And she didn't have anyone in her life to pick up the pieces of her mess, so she fought to the death to hold on to the perfect image, even knowing it was an illusion.

Been there? Do you know what it's like to maintain an image that has absolutely no relationship with reality? To keep up a façade, to wear a mask that in no way reflects what is going on underneath it all?

 The Lord does not look at the things man looks at. Man looks at the outward appearance, but the Lord looks at the *heart.*

We live in a world that applauds masks. Our world adores image. The more perfect the image, the more applause it receives.

After Paris, I had no idea how damaging an "image" was—how making everything look pretty on the outside can often betray the little girl within. I also had no idea how far I would go to maintain the image. The truth is, I wanted to believe the image people saw in the pictures was real too. I was afraid that if I "got real" about all I saw and experienced, it would ruin the image others had of my "glamorous" life. I wanted everyone at home to believe the fairy tale of the girl who went off to Europe and made all her dreams come true—even though it wasn't true.

After two months of stomping the streets of Paris, all I ended up with was a seven-page editorial and cover, and a funky picture of myself in *Vogue.* It rained every day in Paris. There must have been a gazillion models swarming the streets, and there was barely any work. At one casting I met some girls who recommended I go to Greece for the rest of the summer—it was easy to get work there, they promised, and

I would come back with a bunch of magazine pages, or tear sheets as we called them.

They were right. In Athens, I lived in a *pensione* with a bunch of models from all over the world. All of us were there to build our books—our portfolios—so that we could compete in places like Paris and Milan.

The girls there were more average looking, and pay was cheap, but jobs were plentiful. I did a lot of bridal work—twirling in *piazzas*, posing on the steps of castles and by the Mediterranean. I saw a lot of beautiful places, and I racked up pages of myself wearing expensive suits and coats, dripping with million-dollar diamonds, lounging in luxury hotels, and posing with chiseled men on airplane runways; once again looking successful, happy, satisfied. But let's not forget, that is part of the illusion; you would never know by looking at my book the sordid stuff that went on in my life *behind* the camera.

For example, it was common for the morally corrupt photographers to ask me to take my clothes off. Once again, not all photographers were bad people—many were good. But the bad ones usually made very subtle suggestions: "Can you try this outfit?" then "Change into this shirt," and it was see-through. Next might be, "Can you take off the bra? It doesn't look right in this shot," and so on. The girls on the beach in Greece went topless, so some men thought nothing of asking a teenage girl to take off her shirt at castings.

One client actually put a thick stack of money on the table and offered me a bribe: pose nude for one magazine, and he'd give me the next two covers of another. Now these were very famous magazines, and I knew those covers in my book would change my rate from about $1,000 a day to $3,500 a day, quite possibly more. But I also knew it was a trap, so I turned him down.

A few photographers also asked me to go out on their boats to do shoots, which, of course, I wanted to do because I hoped to see the islands. But I found out from the girls at my *pensione* that the photographers only said that to get models out to sea with them. There they would pretend to take pictures while they figured out how to get the models to have sex below deck! I was scared of something like this

happening to me—it had happened to my roommates—so I never
went on anyone's boat!

⁓◡

In Paris, Victoria had warned me to never accept a drink from anyone
in a club, because models were being drugged and disappearing left
and right. But I never guessed that would happen to me on an interview where my agency had sent me.

On the outskirts of Athens, on the coast of the Mediterranean, it
seemed natural when the photographer took me out on the balcony of
his home to see the amazing view. The orange sun was setting like a
flame over the sapphire water, creating a glimmering golden pathway
down the center of the sea. Whitewashed villas lined the shore. He
brought me a glass of chardonnay, which I accepted politely, although
awkwardly, because wine usually was not offered to models on interviews. But I was enjoying the view so much that I sipped the wine
without thought. Watching the water grow deeper, brighter, more
electric, its rippling surface began to relax me. My eyes grew heavy and
knees grew weak. Suddenly I felt like they were going to give way, and
I gripped the railing to brace myself.

He asked me if I was all right, and I told him that I felt strange. He
suggested that we go inside until I felt better, and then he began giving
me a tour of his house.

As we walked, the brown carpet and gray shadows melded in a haze.
He walked us toward his bedroom, but by that time everything was
blurry, and I felt as though I might pass out. When he suggested that I
lie down for a minute until I felt better, I was in a fog and thought he
was being considerate toward me, so I lay down.

My head felt heavy yet cushioned by the softness of the bed. The
feeling was one of floating, my body suspended in space and time, and,
in my mind, gray clouds shifted in a night sky. I fell into a trance somewhere between sleeping and waking. The darkness tried to swallow me,
but I was not completely asleep. I could vaguely feel someone touching
my back. Hands rubbed my shoulders in circles and then fingered my
neck, rubbing the back of my head.

I strained to open my eyes, feeling the hands run down my spine, then up again. Then fear gripped me. I was finally able to open my eyes. It was dark; the air was dank. He was sitting beside me, and his hands were on my neck. His face was shadowed, and his eyes looked like dark pits. But I was still fully clothed; nothing had happened.

With a sudden surge of adrenaline, I jerked straight up. Scrambling off the bed, I darted out of the room toward the front door. It was locked. Struggling with the knob, I could hear him coming toward me. I unlatched the hitch and raced into the wide, empty street lined with mansions.

I stumbled along the road for a long time, looking up at the enormous sky, crying out, "Help me, someone, help me." I'm not sure if any sound even came out. All I felt was a vast emptiness and how feeble and alone I was in this huge world.

I ran for what felt like a long time in the wealthy, vacant neighborhoods on the outskirts of Athens. Then I came around a corner and saw a cab turning through an empty square. Amazed that a cab would be in this area, I ran to it, jumped in, and blurted out my address to the driver. He didn't understand me at first, so I wrote it down, and he nodded.

I lay my head down on the back seat of the cab and slept. I could feel the slobber running down my cheek, wetting the crease of my skin against the vinyl seat, but I could not lift my head or open my eyes.

When I woke up, I was lying on the sidewalk in front of the *pensione*. A hand was nudging me. It was a photographer who lived in the building. I knew who he was because he had just convinced one of the girls in the *pensione* to pose half-naked for him, and then she slept with him afterward.

He had crooked teeth and eyes like a snake. I did not like him; nevertheless, he graciously carried me up to my room and lay me on my bed.

Next I became hysterical—screaming, yelling, crying. Some of the models came in to try to console me, but I told them I only wanted to talk to Trish, my best friend from home. We had been best friends since third grade. She had gone to Nina's with me, and she knew my career. Trish knew my life. She knew the *real* me.

Finally the models helped me place an international call and left me alone once I got through to her. "I was drugged. He drugged me," I sobbed into the phone. Horrified, she talked me through it until I was no longer choking on my tears. She told me I had to come home immediately. But my flight wasn't scheduled to leave for a few more days...and I had jobs until then.

I rocked myself back and forth on my bed until my cries faded to a faint whimper. The blinds on the windows kept in the darkness but shut out the night. Drained, I hung up the phone and slept.

The ringing of the telephone woke me the next morning. It was the photographer for a German catalog that I was scheduled to shoot; I was two hours late. These German clients traveled all over the world shooting for their catalogs, paying $1,000–$3,000 a day, so this was not a job I wanted to miss.

I heaved myself out of bed and opened the blinds; sunlight flooded the room. My head felt heavy and thick. When I got to the hotel where the shoot was located, the photographer yelled at me for being late. The makeup artist covered up the circles under my eyes, the stylist dressed me in women's active wear, and I spent the rest of the day posing by a swimming pool.

 We all need someone to know about the little girl crying beneath the cover-up.

I never told anyone. Back at home, my parents went to the international newsstands and collected all the magazines with their daughter in them. How could I tell them about all the times I had put myself in the way of danger or, more accurately, all the times my agencies had put me in the hands of strangers? It seemed easier to let them believe the girl twirling in *piazzas*, dripping in diamonds, posing for the cameras in city after famous city, was real.

But the truth is, I did want someone to know what was beneath the image. That's why I called Trish. We all want someone to care. Certainly the photographer didn't care why I was late or what was wrong! He had a job to do, and he wanted me with my mask in place. But we *all* need someone to know about the little girl crying beneath the cover-up.

IT'S IN THE WORD

Five years later, when I buckled to my knees sobbing before God, I think I was crying about all this. At the time I didn't know why I was falling apart. Was it loneliness, fear, or rejection? Had I just gone totally insane?

Now I see that it was all of those—every man who tried to steal my innocence, every comparison to other girls, every image that was just an illusion, a lie. The little girl in me just wanted to come out, to get real and say, "This hurts, and I don't know what to do with it. I need someone or something bigger than me to fix it."

In the Bible there is a story about a woman who led a "sinful life" (Luke 7:36–50). When she heard that Jesus was eating at Simon the Pharisee's house, she showed up uninvited. Not even daring to approach him face-to-face, she stood *behind* the Lord, crying.

While Jesus reclined at the table with his host, the woman fell to her knees, sobbing uncontrollably. In shameless abandon, she washed his feet with her tears and wiped them clean with her tangled hair.

As this woman poured expensive perfume on his feet, I imagine her touching the very skin of God and thinking: "What a mess I am! What a mess I've made of my life. All I have to offer you is this tiny bit of beauty I have left—my broken heart, my shame—poured out in this jar of perfume. Nothing else matters now. What everyone else thinks of me doesn't matter. All I care about is what you think, Jesus, only you. Will you wash me clean? Will you wash off the dirt and grime, and polish me with the oil of your Holy Spirit? Will you make me new?"

The courage to get real with Jesus is breathtakingly beautiful. You cannot create this kind of real beauty with makeup, hairstyles, jewelry, or fancy clothes. This beauty cannot be fabricated; it is so authentic it makes us uncomfortable, so raw and real it scares us.

Of course the Pharisee, who was more interested in having a perfect image than a perfect heart, scoffed at the broken woman, thinking if

Jesus were really a prophet, he would realize this shameful woman was a "sinner" (Luke 7:39). Jesus had just finished explaining to the "experts in the law" that he did not come to heal those who are well, but the *sick*. He did not come to save the righteous, but the sinners (Luke 5:30–32). Nevertheless, Simon looked at the woman and automatically thought, "Yuck, look at her! She is nasty. How can Jesus even stand for her to touch him?"

I wonder if the Pharisees really thought they could fool God by making everything look good on the outside. Maybe that's why Jesus shook them up so much, because he could read their hearts. Simon didn't even have to say it; he just *thought* it!

 In a world obsessed with how things look on the outside, God is searching for hearts that aren't afraid to show what they feel down deep.

In the Book of Matthew, Jesus goes on a tirade against hypocrisy, calling the Pharisees "whitewashed tombs, which look beautiful on the outside but on the inside are full of dead men's bones and everything unclean" (Matt. 23:27). In other words, on the outside, they were clean, sparkling white—they wore a perfect mask—but on the inside, their hearts were ugly and rotting. If they were such "experts in the Law," it seems they should have known 1 Samuel 16:7, which says, "The Lord does not look at the things man looks at. Man looks at the outward appearance, but the Lord looks at the heart." The Lord looks at the *heart*.

So did Jesus reject the woman for her reputation? Because she had made a bunch of mistakes? Because her sins were sexual?

No! He looked at her heart, and he loved her just like she was— broken, messy, *real*. Instead of explaining this to Simon outright, Jesus told him a story about two people with canceled debts, saying that the one with the bigger debt was more grateful than the one with the smaller debt (Luke 7:40–43).

This woman also had a big debt; she needed a lot of forgiveness. She had a lot of burdens she was carrying around, like I had. But she was *real*, and her brokenness and willingness to be humble endeared her to Jesus.

The "perfect image" never does it for Jesus. The image that he loves is the one that reflects his own heart.

So why are you afraid to say, "I'm crumbling," or "I'm in a ruin"? Because then everyone will know the image isn't real, and somehow you've identified your worth with the ability to keep up the illusion. But the illusion is only that—a replication, an imitation. The real thing is what is in your heart, what you feel, and what you want more than anything to pour out at the feet of Jesus.

"Perfect" he can't work with; imperfect he *can*. He can't do anything with *fake* either. The truth is, he *hates* fake. But the messy, crumbling, slobbering, mascara running, hair out of place, "I'm a mess and I need you" kind of real is what pulls at God's heartstrings. Why? Because when we admit that we need him, it gives him a chance to be the Father that we have always longed for. It gives him a chance to be our strength when we are weak.

Sometimes we are more scared than we want to admit. Sometimes we are more alone than we want to say. Sometimes we need help and are terrified to cry out for it. When we do not cry out, when we do not speak, we hide. We hide behind a mask, and our truth gets buried.

In a world obsessed with how things look on the outside, God is searching for hearts like that sinful woman's—hearts that aren't afraid to show what they feel down deep, hearts that aren't afraid to break open and bleed a little…or maybe a lot.

The world says real is not beautiful. The world says beautiful is *covering* flaws, not revealing them! But real *is* beautiful to God. And real, as uncomfortable as it may make people feel at times, is beautiful to other people too.

When most people see true remorse, true humility, and true passion pour out, they feel a glimpse of hope. They sense that if they cracked open their heart a bit and were real with others, God could possibly start shining through their cracks too.

The very first book of the Bible says we were made "in the image of God" (Gen. 1:27; 9:6). Jesus, who *was* the perfect image of the living God, was real. He was authentic. His heart went out to people when they were hurting; his hands touched those who had been rejected; and he never pretended to be someone he wasn't.

Do you want to have the perfect image? Then imitate Jesus. Don't imitate the images of our culture. They are only illusions. What is real is everything we see in the woman who fell at Jesus's feet. It is a willingness to say, "This is what is underneath the mask…and I'm not afraid to let other people know it. I'm not afraid to pour out my heart because I know Jesus loves me even if I'm messy, broken, afraid, sorry, and longing.

"He loves me just like this."

"Your sins are forgiven."…Jesus said to the woman, "Your faith has saved you; go in peace."
—LUKE 7:48, 50

The Lord does not look at the things man looks at. *Man looks at the outward appearance, but the Lord looks at the heart.*
—1 SAMUEL 16:7, EMPHASIS ADDED

He said to me…"My power is made perfect in weakness." Therefore I will boast all the more gladly about my weaknesses, so that Christ's power may rest on me. That is why, for Christ's sake, I delight in weaknesses, in insults, in hardships, in persecutions, in difficulties. For when I am weak, then I am strong.
—2 CORINTHIANS 12:9–10

All of us, then, *reflect* the glory of *the Lord* with *uncovered faces.*
—2 CORINTHIANS 3:18, GNT, EMPHASIS ADDED

Chapter 4

THE PERFECT BODY

Eating Disorders, Dissatisfaction, and the Battle for Control

*T*he downstairs toilet is clogged again. I flip on the kitchen light and scan the pantry shelves. Two loaves of whole-grain bread I bought at the street market yesterday are gone; cereal and dried fruit, gone; pasta and the leftovers from Thai on Wednesday, gone. Empty packaging for juice, milk, cookies, and ice cream are all in the trash. I can imagine Shellie stuffing herself in the dark of the night, careful not to wake Nick, her boyfriend slash father figure slash sugar daddy slash enabler slash owner of the apartment where we live.

I imagine her drinking one too many glasses of wine before bed, then waiting until Nick is sound asleep. Then she would tiptoe past my room, downstairs, and into the kitchen. I wonder if she thinks, "Just a taste, just a little," at first. Does she try at first to control herself, or does she actually plan a full-blown, all-night binge?

How does she place the food on the counter? Is it methodically, as she does when I am there, beginning with bread, butter, and cheese, then ending with cookies, cake, and milk? Or is it just a mad, senseless grab, a chaotic shoveling in of food, not really chewing or tasting anything? Does she eat and eat and eat until she can't help but vomit? Then does she go back for another round?

Yes, I know she does. She told me she does.

When Nick comes down, ready for work, he says, "The downstairs toilet is out of order," as if he is saying, "The sun is up."

I nod. It is, after all, shared knowledge. They told me about the bulimia—which is actually a disorder, not a "problem"—within an hour of my arriving at the house. What Nick is doing about it at this point, I haven't really figured out. I have come to despise his icy, beady eyes; his cold, emotionless stare; and his trimmed, neat-as-a-pin presence.

Nick finally leaves for work. I imagine he hates how messy it is. I think he refuses to unplug the toilet for her. Even more, I guess he only keeps her around because she is his perfect prey—helpless, needy, and trying to fill a void within.

I go out for a run—my own answer to modeling insanity. As I whip around the bends of this quaint, idyllic suburb of Sydney, Australia, I admire the sweet flower-potted balconies and white picket fences.

As I run, my thoughts drift back to my arrival in Sydney. I came here in search of safety and beauty. My first summer abroad—in Hamburg, Germany, at age seventeen—was relatively harmless, but the next summer spent in Paris and Greece had somewhat terrified me.

The German companies I had worked for were generally respectful toward models, and I could just as easily work with them in the safety of my own country, so during the summer after my sophomore year, I decided to work from Los Angeles. During that summer and in the summers to *come, I would do a slew of TV commercials—Oil of Olay, Mercedes-Benz, Converse tennis shoes, Taco Bell, Cherry Coke, Vibrance shampoo—and I also filmed a music video and did a lot of catalog work with the Germans.*

But during that summer right before I went to Australia, a homeless man began to stalk me—following me on campus, camping out in the hallway of my apartment building, nightmarishly pounding on my door at night. But he never seemed to be around when the police were called so they could catch him. So when summer rolled around again, I told Mack, my booker, that I wanted to work somewhere far from LA, which I had come to call "Hell-A." I wanted to be in a place that was safe and beautiful. He promised me Sydney was the ticket.

My thoughts are interrupted as I round the bend back to the picket fence that belies Nick's quaint little house and realize that I cannot escape it—the loneliness, the terror within. It seems anywhere you find models, you find a girl empty and wanting.

When Shellie wakes up, her face is puffy—she looks as if she has been sobbing into her pillow all night. I imagine she must cry when the clumps of vomit clog her throat, when the acid burns the lining of her esophagus. Or maybe she lays her head down on the toilet and cries afterward. Maybe the bingeing and purging is how she sobs.

Maybe it is just one long night of sobbing.

Shellie has large brown eyes; a square, clenched jaw; and a wonderful smile. From a farm town in Iowa, she has a low, deep voice that soars high and sweet when she sings. When Nick isn't around, she sits in front of the stereo for hours, teaching herself to play the guitar by ear.

She has dreams for her life—pure, hopeful dreams. But Shellie is caught in the rude reality of a body that refuses to bend to her ideal of perfection—a body sculpted for modeling, a life built on appearances, and the messiness of the flesh—these all plague her. She is the quintessential caged bird, yearning to sing, yearning to fly far and free.

Shellie's natural build is solid, strong, firm. She has muscular thighs; high, round breasts; and a flat tummy. A size 6 on her card, she is more naturally a size 8 or 10— those double digits considered sinful for a model.

When she came to Sydney, the agency set her up in Nick's two-bedroom apartment, where he rented the spare room to models. Another model, who had previously occupied Shellie's room, was sleeping in Nick's bed. When they broke up, Shellie started sleeping in his bed. I arrived about a year later, breaking the cycle. Amazing how our agencies appeared ignorant of the scenarios they set up for us!

Self-centered, controlling Nick is about forty-three; sweet, hungry Shellie is twenty-one. Nick believes Shellie's bulimia stems from finding her father dead in a pool of blood. He had shot himself when she was only ten years old. It seems obvious that Nick is taking up residence in Shellie's little-girl heart, attempting to fill that need for a daddy. But he is a poor imitation—enabling her bulimia, eying every bit of food she eats, and discouraging the use of her angelic talents.

In obsessive-compulsive activity, Shellie spends hours scrubbing floors, dusting, and nitpicking at every last detail in the apartment . . . because that's the way Nick likes it. It is chilling how disconcerted they both become over any small spill, mess, or flaw. She even has certain sponges and rags for the counter, the dishes, and the floor—which I never seem to get right.

What We're Really Longing For

"The" Body: the organized physical substance of an animal or plant, either living or dead; the material part of a human being

The world says our bodies are things to be controlled. They are messy, unclean, and in need of strict regulation. While saying this, the world reminds us that our value is based on how well we can control these messy bodies of ours.

The perfect body, the world claims, is attainable, and it is OK that we spend the majority of our energies in search of it. But trying to make everything look perfect on the outside, for girls like Shellie and for girls like you and me, can be an exhausting, emotionally crippling, spiritually draining, and never-ending task.

With my nudging, Shellie left Nick, and after about a month, I noticed she didn't even miss him; in fact, it seemed like chains instantly dropped from her ankles the moment she turned the key on our new place.

"How was your day?" I asked one evening as I settled in on the floor of our apartment in Bondi Beach. I had been working all day, freezing on the beach, modeling tank tops and shorts while the photographer and crew wore heavy winter coats. I couldn't wait to nestle in with a cup of tea and a blankie and catch up with Shellie.

But now she seemed forlorn and exhausted. She looked at the ground shamefully.

"What happened, Shellie?"

"They sent me home," she said. "I was too fat for the clothes." Then she turned to scrub an invisible spot off the counter.

"No! I can't believe it! You are not fat!" I was livid that they would tell her such a thing!

"Compared to the other girl I was," she said, spinning around. "She was a rail, and everything fit her perfectly. I did one outfit and the clothes were tight, but I got them buttoned. They sent me home after shooting one roll, and I don't even think the photographer had film in his camera."

I had never heard of a photographer sending a girl home before. "Did they know your size? It was probably their mistake."

"The clothes were size 6, and that's on my card. Usually I wear a 6, but they were too tight..."

"The least they could have done is kept you on and paid you for your time."

"They just told me to go home."

"Did they say why?"

"They didn't have to," she huffed. "I couldn't even zip up the second pair of pants. The other girl was so skinny you could see her ribs...and they loved her."

"Well, that's sick, and you know it," I said, having no idea that two years later that would be me. She sat down on the floor while I poured her some tea and rolled us a joint.

"What did you do for the rest of the day?" I asked.

"I don't really want to tell you."

"Just tell me!"

"I went to a pastry shop and had some hot chocolate and a croissant," she said, looking down at the ground shamefully. "Then I went to another shop and had another croissant, and then I went to another one and had three more. Then after I got sick in a Dumpster, I went to another shop and another and another. I ate pastries and doughnuts and candy bars; then I threw up again...all day!" She hugged her knees tight to her chest and said, "I was doing so well."

I prodded her for more information, and as she spoke, it felt as if her voice was coming from a far-off place, a small, young voice that called from beneath piles of rotten trash in Milan, Paris, New York— cries from a Dumpster. "In Milan I used to do it all the time. On the way to a casting I would eat a candy bar in the elevator, then go to the bathroom and throw it up; that way I could go in and try on bathing suits. Sometimes I would go from bakery to bakery, then from Dumpster to Dumpster.

"I remember going to a casting at *Vogue*," she continued. "I hid in a closet, gorging myself on chocolate croissants, and then threw them up in the nearest bathroom. Then I went and got more and did it all over again. My mind was constantly on what I would eat next, where I would get it, and where I would get rid of it."

"Did anyone ever know?" I asked. "Your family?"

"My family is in Iowa, Jen. They only see me in magazines."

"Isn't that the truth!" I thought to myself. Out loud, I asked, "What about your roommates?"

 Has she had the courage to press through the crowd and reach for the Healer? If I cannot find her to tell her, this book is my way to tell you.

"My roommates were models. They were too busy with themselves to notice."

"I get it. Say no more."

But I desperately tried to tell her she couldn't let this business rob her of her life; she couldn't let that photographer take away who she was—an intelligent, beautiful, talented woman. She was an amazing singer, a creation of God even. I pled with her that what her dad did to himself wasn't her fault, and she had to stop punishing herself. If she had to quit modeling to get well, then she should *quit*!

Who cares what that photographer thought! She was *supposed* to have curves; she was supposed to look like a woman; she was not supposed to make herself sick to be a bag of bones. And she had to stop trying to be something she could never be—perfect.

At twenty, I *knew* all that in my head—maybe even in my heart. But a few years later, my mind too would become poisoned by the same lies, and I would find myself hugging my knees tight like Shellie, shaking, burying the tears within me. I too would lose myself in search of perfect.

⁓

"Look in the mirror!" Damien seethed at me, slamming his hand on the table. The plates shook and glasses clinked.

"I don't need to look in the mirror. I am fine!" I said. "I am working every day!"

After graduating college, I had come to Milan. Within the first few weeks, Damien, a French magazine mogul who divided his time between homes in Milan, Paris, and New York, decided to put me on the cover of the premier issue of his newest magazine—barely dressed and starkly thin.

"You look terrible," he said, his espresso-colored eyes narrowing.

"If I look so terrible, then why is my chart so booked up?" I asked proudly. "The photographers obviously don't have a problem with it."

"Well, I do. You must *eat!*" he insisted. "Honestly, *Jenni-fair*, look at yourself. You look like a *man!*"

Tears rose and filled my eyes, and a choking feeling edged my throat.

"I don't tell you this to hurt you," he tried to console, "but to make you see yourself! To see the truth! Really, what would your father say?"

"My father would not be so cruel," I said, pushing away my plate.

I threw the napkin on the table and went to the bathroom. Locking myself in the stall, I wiped the tears away as quickly as they came, ignoring the knocks at the door. I didn't want anyone to see me crying. "I hate him," I said to myself. "I hate him."

When I first met Damien, he seemed so convinced I could become a top model—in fact, he made it his own commitment to make sure it happened. He became my unofficial manager and wanted me to be his "little discovery." He wanted to send me to the shows in Paris, introduce me to the top designers, and get me in the pages of the very best magazines—including his own. But now that I was withering away before his eyes, he seemed to question my potential.

I walked out of the stall and washed my hands, head down. Then for a moment, curious but afraid, I looked up into the mirror to see if what he said was true. What I saw was shocking. My eyes looked like bruised, punctured peaches; my collarbone and shoulders protruded sharply from a sleeveless top. I could even see my breastbone poking through the fabric. I looked away.

Sometimes we do not want to see what other people can see so clearly.

After college, I knew that if I really wanted to work in Milan, I would have to lose those extra pounds. Having just broken up with a college boyfriend, I spent the summer fasting from anything that contained sugar, fat, alcohol…anything that reminded me of what I had lost in him.

Daily I ran like mad on the beach, did yoga, and went to a tanning bed. I got new clothes and new shoes, and began to wear my hair straight. As the plane left Los Angeles for Italy, I had my mind set on one thing: success. And success to me equaled the runway. *Nothing* was going to stop me from getting what I wanted.

A lot of the most famous fashion houses, bottom line, like their girls to look anorexic. Oh, they may not say this publicly, but that is the body type they choose, time and time again. Of course, the designers are only interested in your body—the material part of a human being—and they take absolutely no account for your soul.

When models go to an audition for a big show—what we fondly called "cattle calls"—it is not uncommon for the girls to be required to walk down the runway in nude bodysuits or underwear so they look nearly naked. I have known certain designers who even stand at the end of the runway and point at each girl as she walks by, saying, "No, no, no, no," sending each one off the stage. Every once in a while there is an "OK, yes, you," and then another long string of "no, no, no."

Personally, I starved myself to get the shows. I went for weeks eating rice, carrots, pears; I skipped dinner, then breakfast, sometimes lunch too. I didn't even dare indulge in a cappuccino, a piece of cheese, or a croissant. And I definitely refused to drink milk or eat chocolate, meat, or pasta. I ate "like a bird," as Marcello, my agent, used to say—and he said it as a *compliment*!

The more I could control my body, the less my hundred-mile-an-hour lifestyle bothered me. The more laps I could swim, the longer I could stay in the steam room, the more grueling I could make my runs, then the more I could deny my hunger. The more I could push myself, the more I felt I held the reins of my life and future.

When I needed to rest, I ran; when I needed to sit still, I did sit-ups; when I needed a bowl of pasta, I ate a pear instead. I even got to the point that I feared food that had fat; I began to only eat the fish off the top of the sushi roll because the rice inside was carbs, and any carbs became *evil* to me.

I did not eat nuts because of the fat. I did not eat bagels, cream cheese, cookies, or ice cream—things I ate without reservation as a child—because this was the world of adults, and in this world, you had to be thin. Thin meant controlled. Thin meant accepted. Thin meant beautiful, and beautiful meant loved.

"Eat!" Damien would say a little too loudly at dinner. "*Eat!*"

"No!" would be my response. And the more he pushed, the more I refused.

Even Marcello tried to talk to me about it. "Put on some weight," he would say. "Eat some pasta."

"I'm doing the Armani shows," I would say, "and if Armani's happy with me, you should be happy."

Of course, no one ever dared to address the starvation that was going on *inside* of me. On the inside, I was starving for love, affirmation, and acceptance. I was putting off the image that I had it all together— another mask—but I didn't. If anyone at that time had dared look me in the eyes and challenge me to get real, I would have crumbled.

I missed my family terribly. I was gripping on tight to my own seat belt of control as the roller-coaster ride of self-worth whipped me up and down, upside down, around loops, and through tunnels. It was an almost constant push and pull. One photographer loved how thin I was; another said I was much too skinny. One man would want sex from me, while another wanted me to be his arm candy, his symbol of prestige and worth in restaurants crowded with the fashion elite.

I couldn't keep up the image. I couldn't keep looking perfect all the time. I could do it for a while, but when I didn't have school to go back to—where I was valued for more than what I looked like—and I didn't have dinners with a family who loved me, I began to feel like a material thing again, a *mannequin*.

After walking or working all day, at night I went to the gym. I would do a StairMaster, work out with weights, do sit-ups, you name it. Then I would sit in the steam room for far too long. The doctor at the gym had barred me from steaming because of my low blood pressure, but I would sneak by him and let the fog engulf me. I wanted that weight off, so I would sweat, sweat, sweat until sometimes I became so light-headed I nearly passed out. Then I would get on the scale and see those numbers going lower and lower…and I would feel accomplished.

When I was seventeen, an agent told me I should get down to 125 pounds, which is about 60 kilos. I am six feet tall. My mom and dad were appalled by that—they couldn't figure out how I was going to lose 10 pounds. As I stood on the scale in Milan, the little black arrow leaning toward 55 kilos, I whispered to myself, "There you go. Are you happy now?"

One night I went to the gym to swim for a few hours, something I often did because an agent had told me years ago that swimming was the fastest way to shed pounds. Undressing in the locker room, I put on my bathing suit. While tying the strings of the bikini top, I looked up and saw that I was standing in front of a mirror.

"Look in the mirror," I could hear Damien say.

I looked around to make sure I was alone, which I was.

The mirror was cropped, reflecting only my waist up. So I began to *look*, not in my eyes, but at my body. Turning my head side to side, I patted the underside of my chin; the jawline was lank, the way I liked it. Then I looked at my collarbone, the skin pulled taut over bone. I had absolutely no breasts left. My ribs poked out my sides. Running my hands along them, I felt the rows of sharp bones. My shoulders, which used to be broad, were now small and frail. Then I made myself look into my eyes—red, purple, hollow, deep, and black—there was no light left in them.

I didn't want to see this. It was fine to see myself made-up in proper lighting, makeup, styled hair, and clothes, but to see myself bare…What I had become underneath all that was shocking, ugly, revolting. I looked like a terror-stricken deer, starved and tangled inside.

"What have you done?" I asked my reflection. My eyes flooded with hot tears, my face cinched in pain. I couldn't stand to look at myself any longer.

When I turned away and stepped toward the pool, the wall of mirrors behind me cried out, "Look! Look! Look and see yourself!"

Slowly, painfully, I turned around and saw my reflection. I had no rear left at all, and my back was only a rack of ribs. I looked like those starving children you see in pictures who are famished and screaming from the inside out, emotionally raped from some violence that has ravaged their land.

"My God," I said aloud. "My God."

FROM MY WORLD TO YOURS

Eating disorders are just that: *dis*-orders. There are conditions in which the body has manifested the disorder of life, the confusion, the chaos, the out-of-order, out-of-sequence ways that mark an unhealthy relationship with food and the mirror. They are psychological disorders, not grounded in the reality of the body, but in the arena of the *mind*. The word *disorder* in the dictionary is defined as "a breach of peace." Eating disorders are a breach of peace on the soul, evidenced in a grave condition that wreaks havoc on the body.

Anorexia and bulimia are diseases of approval. We literally destroy our health in our desperate quest for approval. In our deep longing to be affirmed as we are, we challenge our body's natural hungers, thinking that if we deny them, we will achieve the perfection we think will earn us that stamp of recognition in the world. But the "thinness" is an external representation of an inner pain—or a compilation of many pains—that hurt too bad to talk about. We have internalized our pain to a point that it shows up on our bodies.

Certainly our culture promotes anorexia, splashing bone-thin models and actresses all over the pages of magazines. The girls in those magazines are torturing themselves to be thin, and we are emulating them. Or, even more bizarre, the publishers of the magazines airbrush girls who are at a healthy weight to the point that they look unusually thin, giving us one more unrealistic image we can never measure up to. So our culture promotes the cycle, and the cycle is destroying the self-worth of this generation of girls.

Whether we are bingeing and getting obese, starving and getting skeletal, or bingeing and purging in a roller-coaster ride of control, these are equally distant lines of the same triangle. Eating disorders are an outward reflection of an inner sickness. And the sickness stems from the heart at the center of it all: the longing. The longing to be validated, to be paid attention to, to be loved and applauded and heaped with praise is so deep and so wide that it becomes a pit within us. And it is a pit that no amount of food, diet pills, deprivation, or purging can satisfy.

The scary thing is that we can die longing. The pit can swallow us alive. If we don't call for help, it *will* destroy us—body, soul, or both— because the quest for the perfect body has no final destination. Our bodies are ever changing, and they will never satisfy our demands for perfect. *Never.*

For the anorexic, thin is never thin enough. It becomes a competition with the flesh in which she intends to be the victor. But she never wins. In fact, she loses herself in the process.

For the bulimic, she hates her imperfections so much that she blames herself for them. She tries to control, control, control, and then she loses control and the shame eats her alive. So she too cannot win.

The constant dieter, the overeater, the plastic surgery addict—none are ever satisfied! They are all playing a game at which losing is the only inevitable end.

The world has us trapped in a great lie. The lie is: you can have control over your life. You are the one in charge; control is absolutely within your grasp. For girls, the territory that seems most obvious and tangible to control is the body.

The world tries to teach us that the body is not a house for the spirit; instead it is a thing to be controlled. And if you don't like the way God made you, fix it up! The plastic surgery boom is like a voice screaming through a megaphone: "You can have control! You can have perfection! It is attainable! Come, buy, and eat! It is within your grasp!" As if plastic surgery will bring us satisfaction…as if satisfaction can be bought!

In the era of plastic surgery, there seems little emphasis on how the scars within us heal. It's all about the outside, the image, the *projection* of what's real, and not what actually *is* real. But it is the wounds within that are the hardest to heal and the most telling. We are wounded because we have believed the lie that says: Our bodies *are* our *selves.* They *are* the measuring stick of our worth. They define whether we are beautiful or ugly, good or bad. And finally, at all costs, these messy, imperfect bodies *must* be controlled.[1]

In a world spinning out of control, we think if we can just control our bodies, what we eat, and how much we exercise, we will get peace. Yet, for the anorexic, the bulimic, the obese, the starving, the addict— and the average girl or woman—peace has nothing to do with food or exercise. Obsessions with food and exercise, or the lack thereof, are just ways the world tries to get our focus off the only One who truly has control over the universe, the only One who can give us peace—God. The more we focus on food—or the scale or the mirror—as the determining factor of whether we are good or bad, the less we look to the hands of our Creator, our great Healer, our Sustainer, our Provider. He is the One who made us, and only he knows exactly what we need.

IT'S IN THE WORD

When a bleeding woman pushed through the crowd to touch Jesus, she believed that she would be healed (Mark 5:25–28). She had been bleeding for twelve years—something unfathomable to us. A period that lasted for *twelve years*? Clearly there was disorder in her body—a long, exhausting breach of peace—but I wonder more about the breach in her soul.

In her culture, the bleeding meant that she was untouchable. She was dirty, unclean, *stained*. So no one was touching her. No one was holding her through the pain, the cramping, the mess of it all. I imagine each day she woke up dreading the continued blood flow, dreading her dis-ease, her dis-order, her dis-array. It must have been tremendously painful to be considered an outcast, one whom no one wanted, no one touched. The emotional rejection, the shame, the feeling of being unwanted must have been unbearable.

After I did the Armani shows, it seemed that everyone wanted me. I was flying all over the place for jobs. But when my body began to give out—eye sockets dark and desolate; hair turning brown and brittle and falling out in clumps; skin marred with cystic acne; my period long, long gone; stomach protruding and always in knots—suddenly they didn't want me anymore. The jobs began dropping off. Photographers said they couldn't take pictures of my anorexic body, my acne, my depression.

When I went home for Christmas, my worry-stricken mother tried feeding me—chicken, potatoes, vegetables—square meals. At home once again, I suddenly felt hungry and stuffed my face. Then, back in Milan after the holidays, sometimes I got up in the middle of the night and sleepwalked to the kitchen. I mindlessly ate boxes of cookies, more or less in a dreamlike state that I could only recollect foggily the next morning. It's possible that my body was trying to keep from starving. It's also possible I was trying to fill the hunger in my soul.

 Eating disorders are an outward reflection of an inner sickness. And the sickness stems from the heart at the center of it all: the longing.

I bet the pain the bleeding woman must have felt over the rejection got all tied up in the bleeding. The source of her wound laid in the depths of her little-girl heart, a little girl gone innocently into the world, whose body wouldn't cooperate with the rules of her culture. That little girl could not measure up; she could not get clean or find anyone to heal her or to love her. She spent all she had on doctors and only grew worse.

But when Jesus walked through her town, a throng of people pressing into him, she pushed her way through the crowd. She believed that if she could just touch even the edge of his robe, he would heal her. She knew who he was, that he had been healing and setting free souls held captive by uncooperative bodies and wildly disordered minds. She knew he was God come to Earth, God with us.

She approached Jesus from behind. When she touched his cloak, the Bible says that immediately her bleeding stopped and she felt in her body that she was freed from her suffering. (See Mark 5:29.) Immediately her bleeding stopped—she was *instantly healed*! She was set free from the pain of her messy, imperfect, rebellious body.

But Jesus knew her suffering was not just physical, and he wanted to see her face-to-face. "Who touched my clothes?" he asked, knowing that power had gone out from him. While the disciples dismissed his question due to the masses of people, Jesus kept looking for her.

Finally she pushed through the crowd, came to him, and fell at his feet, trembling with fear. Then the Bible says she told him the "whole truth." She *got real, she cracked, she crumbled.*

And do you know what Jesus said to her? Do you know what he called her? He called her *daughter.* "Daughter, your faith has healed you. Go in peace and be freed from your suffering" (Mark 5:34).

She must have thought, "Daughter? No one wants to touch me, and you see me and call me 'Daughter'? What freedom. What healing! What love. What peace."

Inside every girl perfect is a starving daughter yearning to be seen, yearning to be healed and set free, yearning to be full and satisfied, yearning to be loved and given a peace that lasts.

~~～

My initial healing, like the bleeding woman's, was instantaneous. When I realized the perfect nature of Christ's love for me, the kind that loves regardless of appearances, accepts despite failure, and takes me as I am—imperfect, unholy, messy, and lost—when I really took that in, I didn't need to please man anymore. I knew I was more, oh, *so much more,* than the reflection in the mirror, the number on the scale, or the girl in the pictures. I knew that above all I was his daughter, precious to him. He could see my suffering in the crowd. And he *wanted* to see me, touch me. He would not reject or dismiss me, even when everyone else did.

Although my short bout with anorexia came to a close, I spent years afterward trying to undo the damage I had done to my body. I studied nutrition, took masses of herbs, and dealt with a lot of digestive and hormonal problems. I got my period back. Over time, I got my weight back—at first too much weight, then I had to pare back and find a balance. Most meaningful of all, I had chronically feared that I would never be able to bear a child, that I had destroyed my chances of a healthy reproductive system and would scarcely be able to bear the daughter I always hoped for.

But two years after I married my dear Shane, our precious daughter, Olivia, was born. She was eight pounds, thirteen ounces, and radiant with life. Our son, Zachary, at nine pounds, eleven ounces, born eighteen months later, is a strong, hearty, loving child.

Oh, how I have been healed!

The blessings I received for reaching out to touch his robe are beyond the confines of what I could have dreamt that day by the swimming pool. I still have my ups and downs with eating right and exercising regularly, but I am healthy, whole, and well. Twelve years later, I am utterly well.

Shellie, I don't know about. When I last saw her, I was on my way up the coast of Australia for some no-makeup, no-cameras exploring. She was on her way to Cairns to shoot a toothpaste commercial. I could not help but think that as all of Australia saw her square, shiny white teeth pass across the screen, they would believe the lie—that she wasn't hurting inside, that she was well. I knew what they didn't. I knew the truth behind the smile. I knew she had worn away the enamel on those teeth and shot her metabolism to death throwing up in bathrooms and Dumpsters.

I wish, so badly, that I could find her now, for she *was* the bleeding woman. And I wonder, Has she mustered the faith to throw off all those hindrances of the father who left her alone and wandering? The ways men rejected her imperfect body? Has she had the courage to press through the crowd and reach for the Healer? If I cannot find her to tell her, this book is my way to tell you.

‿

Over time, Jesus has become my mirror, the One to whom I go—sometimes shame-filled, sometimes searching, but always face-to-face—to see where I stand and where I should go from here. And every time, no matter how much gunk I'm bringing him, no matter the ways I've messed up or hurt the people I love, no matter how I've been hurt, he always brings the medicine of his Word to heal, offers to bind up my broken heart, and presents me with the possibility of freedom. Most of all, he always calls me "Daughter."

The Father hand knit your body together to house an eternal spirit (Ps. 139:13, 1 Cor. 6:19). When you put your faith in him, he gives you his Spirit to take up residence within your body, which he then calls his temple.

The understanding that your body is a temporary holding place for the eternal Spirit, however, in no way lets you off the hook when it comes to caring for it. Of course you should exercise regularly, eat healthfully, and be mindful of what goes in and out of it. If you suffer from an eating disorder, faith-based therapy and counseling can help. For some, inpatient therapy is a must.[2]

It is a must because you are worth it. You can't be afraid to get real or to get help. You were designed by God with a plan in mind for your life (Ps. 139:16). You must fight for that life and fight for that plan.

One of the greatest travesties of our culture's obsession with thinness is that it downplays the beauty of our talents. If Shellie only had the freedom to sing, her voice could have blessed us with its beauty. I certainly would not be writing if all I could still see were the imperfections in my body.

Did you know that the Bible says if you spend yourselves on behalf of the oppressed and the hungry, God will actually "strengthen your frame"? (See Isaiah 58:6–11.) Maybe we need to put down the dumbbells every once in a while and go to places ravished with starvation. Maybe that would force us to ask ourselves, Why are we counting calories while children beg for bread? Where on earth have we gone wrong?

Do you want a perfect body? Great, you are going to get one. The Bible teaches that when these earthly tents we live in return to dust, our spiritual bodies will be raised glorious with Christ (2 Cor. 5:1–7; Phil. 3:21). Our bodies will be beautiful beyond the reaches of our imaginations; there will be no jealousy, comparisons, measurements, or instruments to measure our fat percentage. Oh, what a relief that will be!

But in the meantime, we remain in the messy world of flesh; we will groan and long for perfect. We are supposed to, because God wants us to *long for him.* The imperfections are there for a purpose—so that we reach for his robe, so that we cry out in the crowd.

In surrendering control, we find freedom. It is freedom to be the girl God made, utterly imperfect yet, at the same time, fearfully and wonderfully made.

For you created my inmost being; *you knit me together* in my mother's womb. I praise you because I am fearfully and wonderfully made; your works are wonderful, I know that full well.

—PSALM 139:13–14, EMPHASIS ADDED

What is seen is temporary, but what is unseen is eternal.

—2 CORINTHIANS 4:18

The *body* that is sown is *perishable*, it is raised imperishable; it is sown in dishonor, it is raised in glory; it is sown in weakness, it is raised in power; it is sown a natural body, it is raised a spiritual body.

—1 CORINTHIANS 15:42–44, EMPHASIS ADDED

Our citizenship is in *heaven*. And we eagerly await a Savior from there, the Lord Jesus Christ, who, by the power that enables him to bring everything under his control, *will transform our lowly bodies so that they will be like his glorious body.*

—PHILIPPIANS 3:20–21, EMPHASIS ADDED

Chapter 5

THE PERFECT LOOK

Fashion, Pride, and Real Beauty

When I walk into the dressing room for the Giorgio show, there are at least fifteen stations of makeup artists, all with Polaroids of my face taped to their mirrors. They are copying the makeup onto each girl.

I had thought it odd the day I was called to the Armani studios and found I was alone—I did not know why I was there until the makeup artist began his work. He used dark, almost black eye shadow with purple and gold highlights; long, thin arches for eyebrows; plum-stained cheeks; lips the color of embers. He curled my hair in golden ringlets and piled them high like a crown, then wove a black satin ribbon like a snake through the coils. Armani examined, suggested changes, then finally gave his approval, taking my hand and leading me to the stage.

As the press photographer snapped pictures, I stood behind the king of fashion and looked bold as a lioness into the lens. Fashion, beauty, the perfect look: was this not it? For that little girl growing up on the stages of Robinson's and Broadway fashion shows, standing still as a mannequin in the store windows at the mall, this was what I

- Photo by Jim Bonner. Reprinted by permission.
- Every effort was made to identify the source of this photograph. If anyone can provide the name or whereabouts of this photographer, please relay this information to Jennifer Strickland, care of Charisma House.
- Photo by Tony Aquilano. Reprinted by permission.

• Photo by Marcelle. Every effort was made to obtain permission to reprint this photograph. If anyone can provide the whereabouts of this photographer, please relay this information to Jennifer Strickland, care of Charisma House.

•• Photo by Leslie Whitlock. Every effort was made to obtain permission to reprint this photograph. If anyone can provide the whereabouts of this photographer, please relay this information to Jennifer Strickland, care of Charisma House.

••• Photo by Nechelle Wong. Every effort was made to obtain permission to reprint this photograph. If anyone can provide the whereabouts of this photographer, please relay this information to Jennifer Strickland, care of Charisma House.

• • • • Every effort was made to identify the source of this photograph.
If anyone can provide the name or whereabouts of this photographer,
please relay this information to Jennifer Strickland, care of Charisma
House.

bionda

The Middle Years: LA, Germany, Paris, and Greece (continued)

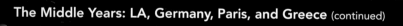

• *Every effort was made to identify the source of this photograph. If anyone can provide the name or whereabouts of this photographer, please relay this information to Jennifer Strickland, care of Charisma House.*

•• *Photo by Alberto Tolot. Reprinted by permission from Jordache.*

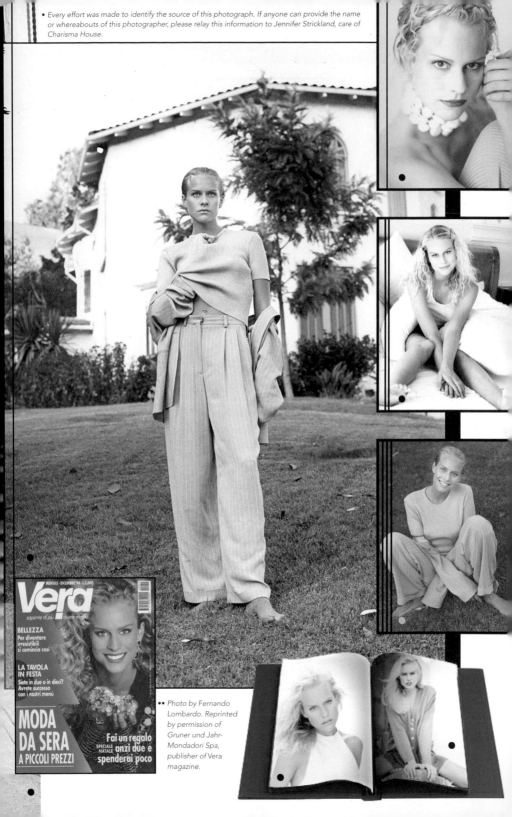

•• Photo by Fernando Lombardo. Reprinted by permission of Gruner und Jahr-Mondadori Spa, publisher of Vera magazine.

Vera
saperne di più vivere meglio

MENSILE · DICEMBRE '94 · L.5.600

BELLEZZA
Per diventare
irresistibili
si comincia così

**LA TAVOLA
IN FESTA**
Siete in due o in dieci?
Avrete successo
con i nostri menu

**MODA
DA SERA
A PICCOLI PREZZI**

Fai un regalo
SPECIALE NATALE **anzi due e
spenderai poco**

• Photo by Angelo Merisi. Reprinted by permission of Gruner und Jahr-Mondadori Spa, publisher of Vera magazine.
•• Photo by Fiorenzo Borghi/Bella/RCS Periodici Milano. Reprinted by permission.

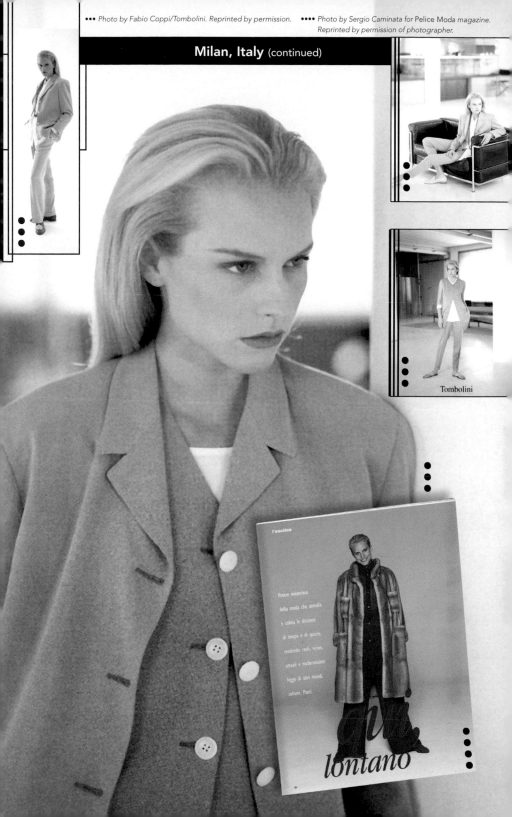

Milan, Italy (continued)

Tombolini

l'esotica

Potere misterioso della moda che annulla e colma le distanze di tempo e di spazio, rendendo reali, vicine, attuali e modernissime leggi di altri mondi, culture, Paesi.

lontano

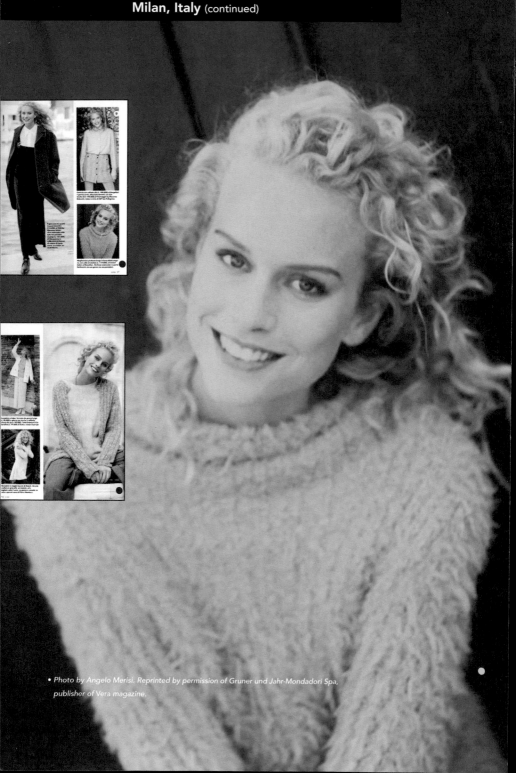

• Photo by Angelo Merisi. Reprinted by permission of Gruner und Jahr-Mondadori Spa, publisher of Vera magazine.

•• Photo by Angelo Merisi. Every effort was made to obtain permission to reprint this photograph. If anyone can provide the whereabouts of this photographer, please relay this information to Jennifer Strickland, care of Charisma House.

••• Photo by Luca Manfredi. Every effort was made to obtain permission to reprint this photograph. If anyone can provide the whereabouts of this photographer, please relay this information to Jennifer Strickland, care of Charisma House.

•• Photo by Daniele Tenconi. Every effort was made to obtain permission to reprint this photograph. If anyone can provide the whereabouts of this photographer, please relay this information to Jennifer Strickland, care of Charisma House.

• Giorgio Armani Spring / Summer 1995 Fashion Show. Reprinted by permission of Giorgio Armani.

• Photo by unknown photographer. Reprinted by permission of Vogue Sposa Italia.
•• Author's personal photo.
••• Photo by Agnes Spaak for Gioia magazine. Reprinted by permission.
•••• Photo by permission.

was supposed to become, yes? A picture taped on mirrors announcing, "Here's the 'look'; get it right."

This is the grand finale of the show season, the crowning accomplishment of the year in fashion. After the fall shows whip through Milan in a whirlwind, the season culminates with this: the Giorgio. While the makeup artists do their magic, the models chat excitedly, strewn all over the floors, plucking their eyebrows, flipping through each others' portfolios, and smoking cigarettes.

Although I am grateful to be here—having been rejected for blowing my walk the first time, but making it after being given a second chance—still, tonight the superficial chitchat of the girls is grating on me; it seems so catty. I feel like I cannot relate to them—they look so flawless. They appear so comfortable with themselves, and by now I should know better.

I am sitting in the corner reading a book Damien gave me and taking notes in my journal. The book is Martin Eden *by Jack London. Based on London himself, the main character, Martin, has this burning, insatiable passion to write. I see myself in him. Even now, I want to be a writer. I remember buying this journal right before leaving for Italy. Attracted by its bright yellow cover, I picked it up in a shop and showed it to my friend, predicting I would "write my first book" in it.*

London writes about Martin:

> *No matter how much he dissected beauty in search of the principles that underlie beauty and make beauty possible, he was aware, always, of the innermost mystery of beauty to which he did not penetrate and to which no man had ever penetrated. He knew full well . . . that man can never attain ultimate knowledge of anything, and that the mystery of beauty was*

no less than that of life—nay, more—that the fibers of
beauty and life were intertwisted, and that he himself
was but a bit of the same nonunderstandable fabric,
twisted of sunshine and star-dust and wonder.[1]

"Sunshine and star-dust and wonder." I write it down
in my journal but know not its meaning. It is time to step
on the stage, and I can feel my heart pumping hot blood
through my body.

"Relax," Armani whispers, his breath hot in my ear. He
presses my shoulders down with his hands. He looks into
my eyes, his gaze twinkling like the Atlantic on a sunny
afternoon, a jeweled reflection of the power he holds in the
world of fashion. Gently, he nudges me.

I step into the center of the runway and turn toward the
"T": the path before me beams with light. The giant tiles of
the stage are lit from beneath. The audience erupts in mad
applause—women adorned with diamond tiaras and fur
coats; men clad in tuxedos, their hair slick and groomed.
The photographers' cameras flash in strobes, and I, dressed
in a flimsy miniskirt and tailored blazer, with a silk scarf
tied around my neck, take the first step.

I am wildly afraid and fiercely bold at the same time—
afraid that I might wobble on those pencil-thin heels that
are so out-of-character for me, yet determined that I will
not; not here, not now. This is what I have worked for all
my life, and I have finally made it.

Rolling my shoulders back and down, I set my jaw with
confidence and let my hips lead the way. Striding up and
down the runway, feeling the draft of soft fabrics rippling
against my skin, my body moves fluidly, without thought,
as if it has discovered a grace it has never known. As I turn
at the end of the "T," the applause roars and my heart flaps
like a caged bird, swelling with pride that I have made it to

this place. I have entered the kingdom of the haute couture, having earned the right to saunter upon that stage.

In the darkness I step off the stage and hurry to the dressing room for the next ensemble. A dresser quickly changes and primps me, then ushers me back in line. Chaos ensues around me; stylists, hairdressers, makeup artists, and show coordinators are scurrying and hurrying about. At the top of the stairs stands Matteo on his walkie-talkie and Giorgio in his regal composure, the prince and his king, crowning each girl with a nod and a touch as she is approved for the viewing audience.

My attention shifts to the models in front of me, admiring themselves in the mirror, clamoring for attention from the paparazzi, who snap pictures of the more famous girls in some behind-the-scenes shots. The models flutter around like hungry butterflies, vying to be caught on film, as if the camera were a sweet nectar that will quench their thirst.

"Oh, dahling! You look simply delicious!" one girl says to another.

"Absolutely divine, dahling, just divine! Love your shoes!"

As the cameras flash pop, pop, pop, *it is as if the lenses of my own eyes come into sharper focus with each snap, and I see the scene before me as it really is, not as I thought it would be. On stage, it is full of color and glitter and hoopla. It is bigger than life. Up there, it feels like glamour has all the power in the world.*

But backstage, everything is strangely hollow, like a black-and-white picture in shades of gray—the power, I realize, is a façade. For the first time, it is as if a veil falls off my eyes and I can see that, despite their exquisite shells, these women are empty on the inside, famished even.

Click, click, click sound our heels as we step forward in line. I am surrounded by models of perfection, decked to the hilt from head to toe, painted up with their chiseled jaws,

glistening eyes, and bony frames, practicing their graceful
turns in front of the mirror. I begin to wonder about these
young women who have made it to such an elite rung on
the ladder of fashion—I wonder if this is all they want for
their lives: to fight for the camera, the money, the top spot
in the fashion world. I wonder if it fulfills them—going
from show to show, city to city, job to job, interview to
interview, approval to approval, rejection to rejection. I
wonder if they have other dreams for their lives. I am sure
they do—they must.

But as for me, right now I realize something deep within,
a realization that modeling has always alienated me from,
a realization that seems the total opposite of everything
that is going on around me. I know I want something
more out of life than this. I want a family, perhaps, love,
a purpose...something...something...I'm not sure what
else, but I know it is more.

It is as if the camera freezes the moment in time; it snaps
and the world is still, and it strikes me that I have had
enough of this world. I have vied for it, fought for it, and
now, I have done it. I have walked it. But oddly enough,
I don't have even a hint of desire to do it again. Most girls
will go onto the next city and the next, doing show after
show, but I suspect I will not.

If it is possible for one to not only feel emptiness, but
actually see it, I believe that I see it right now.

The rounds on the runway blur by me as I move effort-
lessly, almost motionlessly, like someone sailing through
a dark abyss. I hardly have memory of it, except for the
end. Quickly I pull fishnet stockings over black ones and
the stylist buttons a black satin miniskirt around my waist,
cinches a rhinestone bustier around my torso, ties a scarf
around my neck, and straps on stiletto heels. The makeup

artists make their way down the line of models, darkening our lips and eyes for the final walk.

On stage for the grand finale, with our bloodstained lips, shadowy eyes, and jeweled bustiers, we saunter back and forth like a parade of enchantresses, crossing each other in a weaving pattern. Feeling the breeze of the other models' skirts brush my thighs as they pass by, I look into many of their eyes; they are dark, like canyons, black as night, almost frightening in their starkness. Their eyes are deep and hollow—lightless.

It's possible that what I see in them is simply a mirror reflection of what I have yet to see in myself. Maybe it is my own hollowness that scares me the most, the empty life I am leading—so full of excitement and money and prestige and travel, yet so small in meaning.

I will continue to run from this very same feeling in the coming months, until it will finally suck me in and I fall so hard that I land at the bottom of it.

What We're Really Longing For

"The" Look: *a combination of design features giving an attractive, unified appearance*

The runway is the perfect "look"; it is the quintessential picture of beauty in our world. The women stride up and down the catwalk, the fabric falling so delicately from their tender frames, their makeup highlighting their handsome bone structures, their stealth forms moving with the grace of a deer. And we applaud!

Of course we do. The beauty overwhelms us. Mankind has been given a gift—to design, create, and mold the things of Earth into forms that appeal to our love for beauty. Through art and design, we can touch, feel, and experience beauty in ways that inspire and invigorate, even giving us hope that amidst the muck of the world, there is something majestic to be found.

Somewhere along the line, however, we have distorted beauty to the point that it makes most of us feel *un*-beautiful. The average girl—myself included—looking at women on the runway feels largely inadequate in comparison to them. None of us seem to measure up to that "perfect look." Not only do these women have what our world claims is a perfect body— underweight and overworked—the women also have the perfect makeup, hair, clothes, walk, and confident air. Who can compete?

So beauty, as much as it is valued, becomes like mercury for most of us: the more we grasp for it, the more it seems to slip from our hands.

For my roommate Victoria, doing Calvin Klein ads was a way to achieve the longings of her little-girl heart. In the innocence of her early teens, she received the perfect affirmation she needed when a powerful man identified her as desirable. Then she obtained the perfect acceptance when she won the comparison game. Finally, she achieved the perfect image—innocent, sexy, and beautiful all at once; the perfect body— lithe, young, unmarred with flaws; and the perfect look—for Victoria, it didn't get any better than Calvin.

Up on the Armani stage, I had jumped through the same hoops— affirmed and accepted over others by one of the most discerning men in the business. So there I was—what the world says is the perfect image, body, and look.

 Jesus's heart was perfect in beauty; His beauty had nothing to do with the flesh.

Yet, I was unsatisfied. I felt empty within. I longed for more. Although I had done everything I could to get to that league of fashion, I no longer yearned for a better body, a better image, or a better look.

I longed for a more meaningful life. I longed for love, a family, and a purpose. In search of the perfect look, I had missed the essential ingredient in a satisfied life: *meaning*.

Once I obtained it, the runway held very little significance for me. In fact, it seemed more like a game, a parade, a show—which, of course, it was. But that little girl part of me thought it was going to feel more like an "arrival," that achieving a lifelong dream would satisfy me. To my surprise and dismay, it left me longing all the more.

～

"I like this part," the Italian makeup artist said, holding her hand horizontally under my nose and moving it up over my eyes. "But not this part," she said with distaste, moving her hand down my chin. I was on a photo shoot in the mountains of Italy just a few weeks after the Armani show.

The makeup artist explained that she liked my eyes, nose, and cheekbones, but not my mouth. Repetitively, she tried repainting my lips into a shape she could live with.

As I stood barefoot on a freezing cold boulder, wearing a too-tight wedding dress and trying to look like a happy bride, I began to feel the prison of my body. My heart wanted to hike, play, and enjoy the trees and birds and running streams. But I was under the microscope of the camera, the ruthless makeup artist, and busy crew, who were all bundled up in winter coats, trying to achieve that "perfect look" in me.

I was cold—not just on the outside, but chilled completely to the bone.

Once back in Milan, having not shaken that brutal chill, I did another bridal shoot. This time I had emerging blemishes around my mouth. Every time the photographer zoomed in on my face—fully expecting the shot of me to grace the magazine cover—I felt like I was letting him down. He was trying to get that perfect look, and I felt so imperfect, so shameful.

A few days later, I had another photo shoot. Damien wanted to get a simple black-and-white picture of my face for my card, something that would really "sell" me.

"What is wrong with your face?" he asked, as he stood behind the makeup chair where I sat. The sore on the side of my mouth had grown worse, and I had another emerging bump on my forehead.

"I don't know, Damien. I think I'm just breaking out."

"Just 'breaking out'?" he questioned as he leaned in closer. "How old are you, twenty-two? You are not a teenager. No, it looks to me like there is something wrong with you."

He said it could ruin the picture, but they would try anyway so as not to waste everyone's time. I sat silently as the makeup artist worked doubtfully. I hated the imperfections on my face.

When the photographer began zooming the camera in on me, he cussed. My pimples must have glared at him through the lens; they had to readjust the lights. He told me to take a break while they fixed it. I was so embarrassed, my stomach hurt.

When it was all done, he put me in front of the camera again. "If we don't get a good picture out of this roll," Damien cautioned the photographer, "then it is impossible to get one." I noticed members of the crew folding their arms and sighing as they watched me.

I looked down the chute of that lens, diving into the empty worlds that existed there, the very place I had lost myself at seventeen. I looked bare before him. I could no longer cover my insecurity and loneliness.

When we were finished, the stylist dressed me up like a doll and had me pose on a stool for more photos. People later described those pictures as reminding them of a death camp victim—long limbs, pasty white skin, and utterly skeletal frame, with a faraway, vacant stare.

From My World to Yours

One day, we feel beautiful; we are riding on the heights of the world; we are princesses. But then another day we wake up and don't feel the least bit pretty. In this world, our look translates to our value, and that's the problem.

I was fascinated, years after I left modeling, to read about beauty in the Word. In the following passage, the Lord speaks to the women of Zion—the Jewish women of Isaiah's day. As you read these words, picture the modern-day catwalk, what our world calls the "perfect look":

> The women of Zion are haughty, walking along with outstretched
> necks, flirting with their eyes, tripping along with mincing steps,
> with ornaments jingling on their ankles.
>
> —ISAIAH 3:16

It doesn't seem like such a bad thing, does it? In fact, it is much like
what we see walking down the streets of Rodeo Drive in Los Angeles.
Women who are all dressed up and looking good, and *oh, do they know
it.*

They have the jewelry, the clothes, the purses, and the bodies. But
let's not forget that God is looking at their *hearts.* Look at his disdain
for their behavior:

> In that day the Lord will snatch away their finery: the bangles
> and headbands and crescent necklaces, the earrings and brace-
> lets and veils, the headdresses and ankle chains and sashes, the
> perfume bottles and charms, the signet rings and nose rings, the
> fine robes and the capes and cloaks, the purses and mirrors, and
> the linen garments and tiaras and shawls.
>
> Instead of fragrance there will be a stench; instead of a sash,
> a rope; instead of well-dressed hair, baldness; instead of fine
> clothing, sackcloth; instead of beauty, branding.
>
> —ISAIAH 3:18–25

Whoa! Why is he so mad? It seems almost cruel. And if God is
good, then this doesn't seem very kind. He is going to *snatch* away all
their favorite things? Their beautiful clothes and jackets and jewelry?
What has angered him so?

There is certainly nothing wrong with fashion. On the contrary, it
is simply the use of a creative gift God has given man. Made in his
image, man's gifts mirror the Creator's artistic brush and clear adoration for beauty. Just look at a perfect sunset over the crashing ocean,
the sunrise over mountain peaks, dewdrops clinging to autumn leaves,
white pinpricks of stars against an inky sky, or the face of a sleeping
child. These are perfect reflections of a perfect God who obviously
adores the creative act.

God *loves* beauty. In fact, many times in the Bible, he describes how he is going to adorn us with beautiful jewels in heaven. (See Isaiah 61:10; Revelation 7:9; 19:8.) So no, he is not against the clothes or the beauty.

But he *is* against the pride. Proverbs 8:13 says that God hates "pride and arrogance." He hates pride, and these women were awfully showy. They didn't just *have* pretty things; they *flaunted* them, thinking those pretty things made them better than others.

On an even deeper level, they believed they were valuable because of these things—that these things *made them* beautiful—instead of understanding that their value and beauty lay in being who God made them to be *underneath* all that. Their self-worth was locked up in the material goods they draped on themselves.

 Real beauty has nothing to do with the light shining *on* you. It's the light coming *from* you that counts.

God doesn't take too well to that. Why? First of all, he created us for *his* glory, not our own. Like all of his creation, he made us to embody his beauty in the world, to be little mirror reflections of himself. The same way a starry night reflects his power and a mountain vista reflects his majesty, we too are his handmade creations, designed to reflect him in the world.

As reflections of God, made in his image, we are wrong to flaunt the beauty that he created in us for our own prideful purposes. When we do, as the Bible says, it's no longer beautiful to him. In fact, it's downright ugly.

Interestingly, the devil is also described in Scripture as "perfect in beauty." Check out these verses that many scholars believe describe Satan himself:

> You were the model of perfection, full of wisdom and perfect in beauty. You were in Eden, the garden of God; every precious stone adorned you: ruby, topaz and emerald, chrysolite, onyx and

jasper, sapphire, turquoise and beryl. Your settings and mount-
ings were made of gold; on the day you were created they were
prepared. You were anointed as a guardian cherub, for so I
ordained you. You were on the holy mount of God; you walked
among the fiery stones. You were blameless in your ways from
the day you were created till wickedness was found in you.... So I
drove you in disgrace from the mount of God, and I expelled you,
O guardian cherub....Your *heart* became *proud on account of your
beauty,* and you corrupted your wisdom because of your splendor.
So I threw you to the earth; I made a spectacle of you before
kings....So I made a fire come out from you, and it consumed
you, and I reduced you to ashes on the ground in the sight of all
who were watching....You have come to a horrible end and will
be no more.

—EZEKIEL 28:12–19, EMPHASIS ADDED

Ouch! Doesn't sound like fun, does it?

The passion God feels for his creation is humbling. To sum it up,
God *created* Satan perfect in beauty. He was an angel, a created being.
But he wanted to be like God. In Ezekiel 28, Scripture says that in the
pride of his heart he said, "I am a god; I sit on the throne of a god..."
(v. 2). He wanted to sit on the throne of the world. He was not content
to recognize God's place in the order of things.

So in the garden, he appeared to Eve and lied to her, claiming he
was above God and that she didn't have to listen to God; it would be
fine to ignore God's warnings. She could go ahead and eat from the
tree, and, in fact, if she did, it would benefit her (Gen. 3:1–6). As we
know, she fell for it.

Satan traded the truth for lies; he made himself above God.

That is *pride.*

But an amazing thing here is that his heart became proud on account
of his *beauty and wisdom.* God made him with great care—as he made
you. When Satan was still an angel in heaven, God adorned him with
fine jewels. God has also given you your own rare jewels: your gifts,
talents, and blessings.

When you "own" your gifts of beauty and intelligence, considering
them a credit to yourself rather than to your Creator, who gave them
to you, your heart becomes proud. Without even realizing it, your

security can get wrapped up in your looks, achievements, and talents. The next thing you know, you're flaunting something that is not even of your own creation.

This is exactly what I did. I wanted people to know that I wasn't just a model; I always reminded people in the industry that I actually had an education, a mind, as well. While graduating from college on an academic scholarship is a fine accomplishment, the problem was that I was equating my intelligence and beauty with my worth, when, in fact, my worth was based on something so much deeper than that.

When I first came to Milan, I honestly thought that by following the world's ways I would get where I wanted to go—I would get to Oz, and there I would find riches and everything I wanted. But when I got there, behind the curtain, I saw it was a façade. I believed the accuser, the liar, the thief, the one who comes to "steal and destroy" (Rev. 12:10; John 8:44; 10:10). I believed that beauty and intelligence were my "look" and therefore my value. So when that was taken from me— when my skin broke out in horrible acne and my outward appearance began to reflect my inner emptiness—and when my "smarts" couldn't dig me out of the hole I was in, then I had no idea who I was anymore or what my worth could possibly be.

Why was God so angry with the women of Zion?

It was because of their pride, yes, but also it was because he is a jealous God. He wanted them to find their security in *him*. Their worth was tied up in things and appearances that will someday disappear.

As a Father, he saw his daughters directing their gaze at themselves instead of at the One who could give them lasting security, and I believe it broke his heart. In Jeremiah 13:15–17, he says, "Hear and pay attention, do not be arrogant....Give glory to the Lord your God....But if you do not listen, I will weep in secret because of your pride; my eyes will weep bitterly overflowing with tears, because the Lord's flock will be taken captive."

God says if you base your security on the perfect look or on your abundance of possessions, intelligence, and beauty, they will actually become chains that bind you. God loves you so much that he turns his head and weeps bitter tears, as a loving Father would over the daughter he adores.

Today God weeps over the girls and women of this generation because he sent his beloved Son to set the captives free once and for all, and he wants us to truly experience and live out that freedom. But oftentimes, even those of us who call ourselves Christians are still held captive by this ridiculous notion of beauty that the world has placed on us. Too many of us are still prisoners to that quest for perfection.

In Isaiah 61:3, God tells us that he came to bring beauty out of the ashes and joy out of despair. Biblically, beauty has nothing to do with having the perfect look. Beauty is *behavior*.

It's in the Word

When Mary cracked open the jar of expensive perfume and began to anoint Jesus with it, Judas objected. Judas, the one who would betray Jesus. Judas, the one who had been stealing out of the moneybag. Judas, the one who would sell Jesus to the cross for thirty shekels of silver. Judas, the accuser, betrayer, liar, and thief.

"But this money could have been given to the poor," Judas said, as if he could trick the One who reads hearts and minds. (See John 12:4–6.)

"Leave her alone," said Jesus. "Why are you bothering her? She has done a beautiful thing to me. The poor you will always have with you, but you will not always have me. When she poured this perfume on my body, she did it to prepare me for burial." (See John 12:7.) Matthew's account of this same story ends with Jesus saying, "I tell you the truth, wherever this gospel is preached throughout the world, what she has done will also be told, in memory of her" (Matt. 26:13).

She has done a beautiful thing to me—and all the world will hear about it.

What boldness Mary had! What courage to kneel before Christ and pour out her adoration, using whatever wealth she may have had, to pour out the riches of her heart that was filled with love. What bravery to ignore the indignant scorn of her accusers, to unabashedly worship despite their attempts to shame her.

Isaiah says Jesus had "no beauty or majesty to attract us to him, nothing in his appearance that we should desire him" (Isa. 53:2). Yet Psalm 50:2 says, "From Zion, perfect in beauty, God, shines forth. If

God is "perfect in beauty," then wouldn't Christ, the exact representation of his being, be handsome, attractive, stunning, captivating, maybe even movie-star quality? Throngs of people followed him wherever he went; you would think he was at least remotely good-looking!

 Beauty has nothing to do with having the perfect look. Beauty is *behavior*.

Apparently he was not—there was *nothing* in his appearance that would cause people to desire to be near him. Remember 1 Samuel 16:7 says, God does not see the outward appearance; he sees the heart. *Jesus's heart was perfect in beauty; his beauty had nothing to do with the flesh.*

In fact, Isaiah says, when Jesus was on the cross, he was marred beyond human likeness; people turned their faces away from him in disgust, in horror! (See Isaiah 52:14.) Yet the cross is the ultimate act of perfect beauty—or rather, perfect love—one can find on Earth. I challenge you to find something more profoundly perfect than the cross. It brings you perfect mercy and perfect forgiveness, and it is the perfect sacrifice that guarantees you an "eternity of perfect": heaven.

Why did Jesus defend sweet Mary in her attempt to anoint him? Because he saw in her the perfect image, the perfect look: a heart pouring out her boundless love.

He saw God's real nature reflected in her. She was a little mirror reflection of himself—of he who washed the feet of others; he who touched, healed, and reached out despite the bitter hatred he incurred; he who in his final breath took his great love for us on his own body as *a sacrifice.* He loved to the point of death. That is the true nature of love: sacrifice, giving beyond the point that it tears your heart in pieces.

I don't know what label Mary's outfit bore that day. I don't know the cost of her shoes or her purse. I have no idea if she wore any makeup; if her hair was styled and sprayed; if she was overweight, underweight, pudgy, or toned. Jesus made no note of it. He only saw her heart, and in her heart, he saw *his* heart. He saw a heart so full of real beauty that it couldn't help but spill out in her behavior.

The Bible says a beautiful woman who shows no discretion is as pretty as a ring in a pig's snout. (See Proverbs 11:22.) That's an apt reply to the world's definition of beauty, which has *nothing* to do with discretion—choices, behavior, or speech—but *everything* to do with the outer shell. Another translation of this verse in Proverbs says, "Like a gold ring in a pig's snout is a beautiful face on an empty head" (THE MESSAGE). Ha! It's true. Having the perfect look on the outside isn't a recipe for real beauty and has nothing to do with our worth.

That day in front of the camera with Damien, I was no less worthy and beautiful than I was on the first day a photographer ever shot me—when my skin was flawless and body balanced. The sores on my face didn't change my value any more than changing clothes could change who I was beneath them.

Beauty, according to Proverbs, has nothing to do with capturing a perfect look; it is based on the discretion you show in your life. *Discretion* is what you say and do, the choices you make, the way you conduct yourself. When you speak poorly of other people, gossip, cuss, lash out in anger, flaunt your body, or share your sexuality outside of marriage, the beautiful shell on the outside gets lost on you.

Real beauty—not only to God but also to people—comes from the way you treat them. The way you look them in the eye. The way you care about the struggles of their lives. The way you speak kindly to others. The way you hold out your hand when a friend has fallen and needs help. Beauty is *grace.*

Real beauty has nothing to do with the light shining *on* you; it's the light coming *from* you that counts. For me personally, it wasn't until Christ came into my heart and began to shine his light from within me that I began to find satisfaction apart from my looks. Having never felt satisfied with my appearance, I began to realize it was the choices I made and the way I treated others that truly made me beautiful; it was the woman *within.* Beauty does not come from outward adorn-ment, as 1 Peter 3:3 tells us. Instead it comes from your inner self, the unfading beauty of a "gentle and quiet spirit," which is of great worth in God's sight.

These days I care more about being of great worth in *God's* sight than in *people's*. In the end, the fancy clothes and makeup and jewelry will be gone, so our security better not be tied up in them. The gentle, quiet spirit that is so precious to God will be all that is left. That spirit is not our own; it is God's Spirit within us.

Want the perfect look? Great, the Bible has the formula: "Clothe yourselves with compassion, kindness, humility, gentleness and patience" (Col. 3:12). There you go—the perfect outfit. Try it on every day, and see if it actually gives you a look that lasts and that transcends fashion and age. Be daring! Be different! Become like the holy women of the past who used to make themselves beautiful by their spirits within.

This doesn't change, by the way, the fact that I'd love to have a closet full of perfect outfits. I'd also love to have perfect skin. But I don't, so these days I present myself the best I can: I eat right, exercise, dress as well as can be expected, and do my best to keep up with the fashions. But my security is not wrapped up in that anymore.

My security rests in knowing deep down within me is a perfect beauty—not because I *look* perfect, but because my heart has been filled with Christ's perfect love.

One of the most amazing things that changed my life was reading Song of Solomon. I discovered this while reading Beth Moore's phenomenal Bible study *Breaking Free*.[2] Chapters 2 and 4 are where Jesus describes the moment when we see him again one day:

> Arise, my darling, my beautiful one, and come with me....Show me your face, let me hear your voice; for your voice is sweet, and your face is lovely....How beautiful you are, my darling! Oh, how beautiful! Your eyes behind your veil are doves....Your lips are a scarlet ribbon; *your mouth is lovely....All beautiful you are, my darling; there is no flaw in you....*You have stolen my heart.
> —SONG OF SOLOMON 2:10, 14; 4:1, 3, 7, 9, EMPHASIS ADDED

That, my friend, is a love like no other. After all those times I was told I should change my lips, my mouth didn't look quite right, or my face wasn't good enough, to know that he says I am "all beautiful," there is "no flaw" in me, and he *wants* to see my face brings me to tears.

That is how he sees you as well—utterly beautiful—because he made you, and he can't wait to see *you* one day, face-to-face.

Therefore I tell you, *do not worry* about your life, what you will eat or drink; or *about your body, what you will wear.* Is not life more important than food, and the body more important than clothes? Look at the birds of the air; they do not sow or reap or store away in barns, and yet your heavenly Father feeds them. *Are you not much more valuable than they?"*
—MATTHEW 6:25–26, EMPHASIS ADDED

Our lives gradually become *brighter and more beautiful* as God enters our lives and we become like him.
—2 CORINTHIANS 3:18, THE MESSAGE, EMPHASIS ADDED

Clothe yourselves with the Lord Jesus Christ…
—ROMANS 13:14

Charm is deceptive, and beauty is fleeting; but a woman who fears the Lord is to be praised.
—PROVERBS 31:30

Chapter 6

THE PERFECT DREAM

Money and Success

arbie! Barbie! Te amo, Barbie! We love you!" The children cheer as they float with me in a mob down the aisle. Their big, black eyes set in olive skin look up at me from just three feet down. They reach their hands up, begging for my touch. There I am: Barbie, in real life. Beauty, success, perfection, a girl's dream personified...a princess. It's Barbie's birthday, and she has come to Gardaland just for them. I am as excited as they are.

Damien, on the other hand, is enraged at my agency's decision to send me to Verona to represent the doll. He wants me in Paris to do the shows. He wants me to do what he wants me to do. But I am a puppet on the agency's strings, so I find myself in Verona, at Gardaland, Italy's version of Disneyland, for the thirty-fifth anniversary celebration of Barbie. Why? Because the job pays more than going to Paris.

The makeup artists spend hours caking on the makeup, covering the dark circles under my eyes and a few cysts now protruding on my cheeks, chin, and forehead. The stylists scamper to cover my sharp clavicle bones and meek shoulders with pink straps for the dress; they put on long, white satin gloves so no one will see my bony arms.

All gussied up in the taffeta gown, with layers and layers of light pink satin and rose-colored crinoline cascading to a hem of silver garland that brushes the ground, I fit the bill. I have become the doll that I played with as a child; the doll with impossibly slight measurements; the doll without flaw, at least on the outside.

Of course, within the human doll, a soul is imprisoned—a soul that longs to get out of that shell and run free; that aches and pushes and writhes in the confines of that plastic body, longing to be loved, not covered up with false layers.

But tonight, my hair is in a bouffant of soft, molded curls, topped with a huge hot pink bow, just like the ones you see on birthday presents. The children are running at me, calling, "We love you, Barbie!" There are hundreds upon hundreds, maybe thousands, of children. They are racing toward me, calling, pawing, and pleading with me. They just want me to touch them; they want to brush their soft little hands on the satin of my gown.

Don't we all hope there are princesses in the world for which every fairy tale comes true? Don't we all want a brush with beauty? Bending over, I hold their hands and return their sweet embraces. I am laughing now, and tears well up in my eyes. I am the one who sees the beauty here. I am the one who gets blown away by it. They think it is them; it is their privilege to touch me, to see me. But it is the opposite; the privilege is mine and mine alone.

When I reach the front of the auditorium, most of the children let go, but a group of them keeps clinging to me as I climb the stairs to the stage and take my place at the microphone, beaming and waving at the crowd. Who would have known that last night I tossed and turned in bed under violent dreams? Who would have known how cold my chills were that morning as I stood under the scalding shower, sleepless and weeping from a loneliness that had no voice?

As some of the children float right onto the stage with me, I speak my line into the microphone: "Grazie! Tutti aspetterò nel mio padiglione." *I hope that I pronounced the last word correctly, as the director is worried I won't say it right.* "Thank you. I will be waiting for everyone in my pavilion." *The children and their parents erupt in applause. I feel more affection than I have in eons.*

"A stupid decision!" *Damien had snarled at me when I told him I was taking this job.* "Barbie? You are going to go be a doll when I arranged for you to be in the shows in Paris for one of the top designers in the world, who is also my personal friend?"

"Damien, it was the agency's decision, not mine!"

"Stupid girl!" *he said with disdain.* "You should have more control over your career!"

Was he angry about the shows or the fact that he tried to seduce me last week and I didn't let him touch me?

Nothing happens by accident.

I spend the day in the pavilion, surrounded by Barbie memorabilia, while droves of children wait in long lines to get a picture with me—or rather, with their doll. They sit on my lap; they smile at me, hug and kiss me. And one by one by one, I sign their books and take pictures with them, just as they would do with Cinderella or Sleeping Beauty.

When the client asks me if I want to take a break to eat, I tell her I can't stop; I don't want to lose one precious moment with even one child. Too valuable is each bright smile; too dear is each child's eye that is not yet reddened, tired, or surrounded with lines; too precious is their fresh, clear, unadulterated beauty.

The payment I receive for the time spent with these children pales in comparison to what it has done for my heart. They have planted a seed of hope in me that, possibly, becoming a "top model" might not be my destiny. It is not my destiny to be plastic.

When I return to Milan, I am changed. I begin to have moments when things become more real to me. Barbie, Sleeping Beauty, Juliet, Cinderella, Snow White... they are fairy tales; they are legends. They are not real! But in the disguise of one of those fairy tales, I realize that there is more to life than this.

Touching lives, touching hearts, touching souls; yes, that might be the path that God has for this little-girl heart stuck in this big-girl body.

What We're Really Longing For

Dream: *a strongly desired goal or purpose; something that fully satisfies a wish*

Every little girl has dreams in her heart. Many of them are planted by the fairy tales we learn when we are young. We dream of someone seeing us in our loneliness and believing we are beautiful. We dream of someone sweeping us away from the drudgeries of life, rescuing us, and promising an everlasting love, a hope, and a happily-ever-after. We anticipate that when the dream is fulfilled, we will be satisfied at last.

The *American* dream is that we can all make this happen for ourselves. Women's liberation taught us that this dream is possible *without* the fairy-tale prince who sets it all in motion. So instead of the dream coming to us, as it does to the princess, our culture has taught us to *chase* the dream. Somewhere along the line, however, the ideals of wealth, success, and even fame have replaced the prince. The world's theory then teaches us: if there is no prince, then these *things* will bring fulfillment. But can they really hold a candle to the love needed by our little-girl hearts?

Dreams can be forgotten, lost, or stolen. Sometimes they can simply be overshadowed by the dreams others have for you. I remember a phone conversation I once had with my mom. I had just returned to my apartment in Milan after that horrible photo shoot with the white bed, the crimped hair, the fake eyelashes, and the pot-smoking photographer and his crew of coyotes. I didn't yet know that I had been unknowingly watched by the men behind the window.

"Hi, Mom," I said into the phone, careful to guard my voice.

"What is it, Jenny?" she asked. I was disconcerted, and Mom could tell.

Burying the truth as usual, I told her how much I was working, being chosen for the cover of Damien's magazine, an upcoming spot in the bridal Italian *Vogue*, a TV commercial I just landed…

"That's so wonderful, honey. We are so proud of you."

"But what does this all mean though, Mom, without *love*? Without anyone to share it with me?"

"Well, you have people at home who love you honey," she tried to reassure.

"But there's no one here, Mom. I'm alone. I don't know how long I can do this."

"Any girl would give her eye teeth to do what you are doing, Jenny. Millions of girls all over the world *dream* of being a model. And you're very successful at it."

I couldn't speak the truth, and she couldn't hear what I was trying to say beneath the layers. I was looking for something *real* in a world of masks, something to fill this longing in my heart. But she didn't understand.

Of course I should have told her all that had been happening. I should have been strong enough to say, "Mom, these clients are trying to get me to take my clothes off. These older men are trying to get me to have sex with them!" I should have been strong enough to get real, but I wasn't. I was still that little girl with the dream of doing the runway, and even more, the desire to make everyone proud of me. And now that I was in the spotlight, I was supposed to be happy.

After hanging up the phone I buried my face in my hands and cried. It wasn't until years later that I could fully understand where Mom was coming from. As a child, she wasn't allowed to do things other little girls around her enjoyed doing—playing, dreaming, pretending, imagining. So as a grown woman, she wasn't about to let me pass up what she believed was the "perfect dream." I think she wanted to believe the dream was possible, and that it would be worth the moment of loneliness I was having, if I just stuck to it.

My very few calls home during this time continued to be met with confusion and misunderstanding. But the good news is, they drove me to my knees. That night after the phone call with Mom, I knelt on the wood floor beside my bed. The sharp pain of my bone-thin knees against the hard wood shot through my body, and the tears began to fall. "Thank you for my success, God," I finally said. "Thank you so much…but all the money and magazines and clothes don't mean anything to me without love. Please, if you hear me, send me someone to love. I beg you, that's all I need."

~~~

After the Armani show, everyone seemed to want me. My career took off at a pace I could barely handle. I had designers, photographers, agents, and clients pulling at me from all directions. I would go into the agency to discover that my chart was booked solid—some days, I had several options on a day's work because two or three clients requested me *at once*. I had never had this kind of demand on my career before.

While Tina was packing up to leave town for lack of work, I was going from job to job, studio to studio, auditorium to casting room, to the apartment to sleep, only to wake to another day of doing it all again. I was working so much I often didn't even have time for interviews—those had to be squeezed in *after* work. Talk about building my book—I was doing magazine editorials, TV spots, campaigns for good designers for great pay. I even had international agencies flying me between Milan and the United States for catalog work—all expenses paid! No one had *ever* been willing to do that before.

It was so exciting. With school no longer interrupting my stint in Europe, it seemed I could soar to become the "top" model Damien wanted me to be. I would no longer be just a regular "working" model as I had been all these years.

There is a lot of money to be made in this business. Girls can land multimillion-dollar contracts in the blink of an eye. But for the vast majority of models, that never happens. At this point in my career, I was being considered for a major print campaign with Giorgio Armani, and I knew what that meant: money, money, money.

But life moved at such a frantic pace. Every day was a routine of putting on the mask created for me by makeup artists and stylists; every day dressing up and pretending to be a different person. One day I would be young, carefree, and innocent; the next day mature, sexy, and seductive; while the next I would be classy, professional and dignified.

Every day I had to be whoever *they* wanted me to be. After a while, I began to wonder who on earth the girl was beneath the get-up.

I have often heard celebrities like Oprah talk about the detriment of "not knowing who you are" when you reach a certain level of success. They tell how success can disillusion and even destroy you because, when you get into the business or you first become successful, you don't have a strong sense of self-worth. This is what happened to me.

The pace took its toll. Physically, my body became more and more skeletal. I was unable to stay warm; I always felt freezing cold. And I hadn't menstruated since I came to Milan. The acne grew worse every day; even my hair began falling out in clumps, and my legs began bruising from any small bump. Emotionally, I became completely bankrupt. That trip to Venice took the wind out of my sails completely; when Damien's son took from me what was mine to give, as I said before, it was the beginning of my end and the end of my beginning. It was the final nail in the coffin of the little girl who once was. So this was just another mask I had to wear—the mask that says, "Nothing in me hurts. It's all good. All smiles."

The longing for home, school, friends, and family—the longing for unconditional love—was a deep pit within me. I literally began to daydream of being *anywhere* I didn't have to look perfect all the time, *anywhere* a mask wasn't necessary. I daydreamed of having frizzy hair, a pooching stomach, or wearing an outfit that wasn't quite right— and that being OK. I daydreamed of crying from the hurt and it not mattering that my eyes got red and swollen from the honesty of it all.

Deep inside we want someone who won't
leave us for any reason or excuse. We want
to know that if everything unravels, we will
have someone who knows our hurts and is
willing to tend our wounds.

I daydreamed of *freedom*, childhood freedom—to laugh, to play, to just be me. And at the core of my heart, I didn't really dream of becoming the top model that everyone around me seemed so hopeful I could be. Beneath the masks I wore, I wanted a better fairy tale, the one where I was known, seen, and loved for who I was underneath all the layers of makeup and hairdos and pictures and opinions of men.

Once again I felt a dire need to get away from the city, the smog, the craziness. I needed to breathe, recoup. I decided to go to the *bosquo* for the weekend. *Bosquo* means "woods" in Italian, and I chose to go to Como, a mountain lake just outside of Milan. Always drawn to the mountains, I hoped getting away would help clear my head.

Como is a very peaceful place. I stayed in a little bed and breakfast where a beautiful old *signora* cooked for the guests. The first morning I was there, I sat at a window overlooking the lake and sipped some hot tea. Through the window, I saw a group of four dogs playing on the shore, who then tumbled through the door ready for their breakfast of leftovers the *signora* scooped in their bowls. One of the dogs, a little white one with a brown face and a white wishbone of fur on the bridge of her nose, ignored her food bowl and ran right up to me, cuddling next to my leg and licking my hands.

"*Oh, sei bellisima!*" I said to her. "You are so beautiful!" I had heard those words countless times since I had come to Italy, and now they came out of my mouth...about a *dog*!

"*E 'stata abbandonata,*" the *signora* said. I knew enough Italian to realize she said the dog had been abandoned.

But then the *signora* began to rattle off the story. I couldn't follow her, so her daughter translated. A few weeks ago, a woman had brought the dog to the hostel, looking for a home. "I already have three dogs," the *signora* had told the lady. "I cannot take any more." A few days later there was a rainstorm, and the little dog came back without a collar, drenched and scratching at the door. The woman had abandoned her, and the dog had remembered the warm hostel. Now the *signora* was looking for an owner.

I never had a dog in my life. But immediately I was drawn to her. She had kind, searching, brown eyes.

"You want her, don't you?" the daughter asked me that night as she served me the best spaghetti I'd ever tasted. I was taking small, cautious, fearful bites when the kind *signora* began handing me thick chunks of white bread, using it to lap the sauce from the bowl and handing it to me, telling me I had to learn to eat, that it would help my shivering.

As I threw out my caution and took a few hearty bites, it was as if blood began returning to my limbs. My eyesight immediately improved. I began to feel like someone was resuscitating me.

Of course it would be ridiculous for me to have a dog while I was modeling in Europe. I knew that.

But she had been abandoned. She was alone. She was cold and hungry.

That night the *signora* took me out to her garden and showed me the red Roma tomatoes and vibrant basil she used to make her spaghetti sauce. She had lemons and oranges and olives and flowers of all kinds growing in her garden. Oh, how it made me long for my own grand-mother at home.

Patiently, she told me how she grew each one, and she then brought me in her kitchen and taught me how to make the delicious sauce from scratch: first the olive oil, then the diced garlic and onion, sautéed until the garlic was gold and the onion clear, then the purest tomato sauce, the salt, the basil, the oregano. I had so much fun. It was like coming home, like coming back to what mattered.

The *signora* asked questions about my mother and grandmother, obviously considering it very odd for a young woman to be so far away from her family. With every stir of the sauce, it was if she was saying to me, "Now, you can go home and share this with the people in your life who really matter."

The morning I checked out, the *signora* picked the little dog up and handed her to me. "*Un piccolo regalo per voi,*" she said. "A little gift for you."

Although I knew it was not going to be accepted by anyone, I brought the little dog back to the city with me and named her Bosquo, after the woods from which she came. She was as out of place in Milan as I was. Damien later described her as the saddest dog he had ever seen.

She lay on my bed like a wet mop.

But the stillness of Como didn't endure for either of us. When I got back to Milan, my schedule was just as fast-paced as it was when I left. I had to board a plane for Miami. Since I would be gone nearly a week, I gave some money to my new roommate, a seventeen-year-old girl who just arrived from who-knows-where, so she could take Bosquo to the vet for me and care for her.

~⊙

The German photographer was ranting and raving. I couldn't figure out exactly what he was so upset about. Yes, he had flown an entire crew from Germany, and me from Milan, to Miami so he could shoot on the white sand beaches against a clear blue sky. And yes, there was a horrific storm raging outside, so he had been forced to rent a studio and shoot pictures in front of a fake backdrop of a painted beach. So, yes, we were all stuck inside and it was costing him a lot of money, but I didn't see that as a good reason for his angry outbursts.

I sat in front of the camera, trying to pose how he wanted, trying to ignore the fact that he was growing more and more agitated. Finally he exploded at the crew, screaming and yelling. I feared that he was yelling about me, that he could see through the makeup and hair, that I was terribly lonely beneath it all. Maybe I couldn't fake it anymore.

Angrily, he sent me back to the makeup chair. While the makeup artist kindly tried to touch up my face, I begged him to tell me what the photographer had said. But he was a nice person and really didn't want to tell me.

"He is a horrible person," the makeup artist said, hoping to leave it at that.

But I persisted, and finally he gave in: "The photographer said you are insecure, anorexic, and depressed. He said you have acne, that you are ugly, that he hates you, and can't take pictures of you."

"Wow," I said, swallowing hard and looking down at my hands. A pit formed in my stomach. I fell silent.

That night the entire crew went out to dinner for the photographer's birthday, but I was not invited. He couldn't even stand to have me at his table.

Alone in the hotel room, I called my brother Greg.

"I don't know if I'm cut out for this," I said.

"What are you talking about?" he asked.

"Modeling!" I insisted. "I'm not cut out for modeling!"

"Sure you are, Jen! You've been cut out for it your entire life!"

I tried to explain that I would rather go barefaced and work in a flower shop and make minimum wage than have to look perfect all the time. Every day on my way home from the metro in Milan—usually made up with thick makeup and too much hairspray—I passed a flower shop. The girl behind the counter wore no makeup and looked so happy. She had a dog curled up at her feet underneath the table, and people who stopped to greet her seemed to know her and care about her. Her life seemed *simple*.

Greg tried to talk some sense into me, pointing out how rare it was for a girl my age to make thousands of dollars a day getting flown all over the world and traveling throughout Europe, while he was in a cubicle working his tail off in downtown Los Angeles.

I knew what he said was true. I knew that I sounded ungrateful, crazy even. And I knew that Greg simply longed for the undeniable opportunity for adventure that I had.

We ended the phone call.

It hurt that he didn't hear me, but I didn't blame him. I should have told him what that photographer said about me. I should have told him everything! Greg—or my parents—would never have wanted anyone to treat me the way those people did.

But I didn't tell. I ate a few bites of a dry, tasteless salad and went to bed. For the next four days, I endured the photographer's scorn while he fawned over the other girl on the job, either ignoring or deriding me during our few exchanges.

I never ate meals with the crew. The funny thing is, when I looked good, they *always* wanted me at their table.

～

I returned to Milan, only to find that my roommate had skipped town with the money I gave her to care for Bosquo and had left the poor dog shivering and alone in the dark of our hollow apartment.

"If you are going to fly, fly now, fly fast," Damien said to me over a very strained dinner. He looked down at my little dog with disdain. "What you really need is a man, but instead you have stolen this dog from the *bosquo*! It is disgusting." I think he was angry that I was not becoming what he wanted—the trophy in his right hand.

I chased back the tears.

What I needed was love, not a man.

I decided to fly. I booked my plane ticket for Christmas. Bosquo was my carry-on. When we landed in the States—looking like we'd been through a war—my father picked us up. He was obviously struck by and not sure what to say about my gaunt appearance and the fact that I was traveling with a small, forlorn dog.

We didn't speak much about why I suddenly jumped on a plane and came home. I could not even begin to explain the history to him. So I clenched my teeth shut and only made little comments here and there about not really wanting to go back. He knew, though, that I had some big money jobs lined up over there, including the upcoming spring Armani shows.

After I had been home for about ten days, he said, "Jennifer, *why* don't you want to go back?"

I gave him several excuses: the ugly city, the cars, the smog, the angry people…

But he pressed me: "There was all of that in Paris," he said, "and in Athens, and in Los Angeles, and you lived there."

"The men," I said, almost too quietly for him to hear me.

"What?"

"It's just, there are all these older men…" I hesitated.

"And?" he prompted.

"Nothing, Dad. I—I just—I *do not* want to go back!"

I walked away and went to my room. We didn't speak of it again. Instead, he encouraged me to talk to Nina.

It was the least I could do. After all, Nina Blanchard, the empress of the most historic modeling agency on the West Coast, had offered me my first Hollywood contract at age seventeen. Now that I was finished with college, she was expecting me to go work in New York for the empress of the East Coast, Eileen Ford, her counterpart and personal friend.

"You're kicking up a storm over there!" Mack, my booker, said when I walked into Nina's. "Armani! What's up with that? Come on, baby!" He whistled, giving me a high five.

I made a beeline for Nina's office. We had a special relationship, marked by a rare integrity. When I was seventeen, I stayed in her home, and, more significantly, I always felt that she had my best interests at heart. When I wanted to keep modeling in Hamburg, Germany, and not return to start college, she wouldn't let me. She told me that I would never make real friends in this business. In college, she said, I would make lifelong friends—and she was right. Even when I had a possible offer to do *Sports Illustrated* for the first two weeks of my freshman year, she wouldn't let me forsake or even delay my education. She was a class act. I wonder if there are agents like that anymore.

I followed Nina back to her private office.

"What's going on, honey?" she asked, looking me straight in the eye.

"I'm thinking of getting out of the business, Nina," I said.

She was surprised.

But then I told her about the struggles I was having with the superficiality of modeling, my skin, my weight.

"You've always known it was superficial, Jennifer," she said, "And that's always bothered you. And the skin, well, that'll kill ya," she said. "There are plenty of girls out there with perfect complexions, so they'll just pick someone else." She paused as if choosing her next words carefully. "What's your daily rate now?"

"Fifteen hundred to two thousand dollars a day."

"All right, here's my advice. Don't get out just yet. Go to Germany—do Munich, Hamburg, Berlin. You know that's where the money is. Make as much money as you can, milk the business for all it's worth, then get out. Go back to school if you want, travel, do whatever—you don't have to go to New York. But stick it out one more year."

I flashed back to our meeting when I was seventeen, the Hollywood contract sitting on the desk between us. Mom and Dad were perched on either side of me, the three of us hanging on her every word. We had always heard that if we really wanted to know if I could make it in the business, go see Nina. She had a reputation for telling girls, bottom line, if they would be successful as models or not.

She had big ideals for me. Along with a popular entertainment show, she named me "face of the '90s." She believed I could be a "top model." But she wanted me to understand the business that she knew so well, and I never forgot the advice she gave me that day.

"Remember two things," she had said, her eyes darting from me to Mom to Dad and back again. "First, your beauty is not a credit to you but to your parents, rather their DNA! And second, and probably most important," she said, tapping the point of her pen on the contract, "some day, take the money and run…run far and run fast…and never look back!" She laughed a laugh that came from deep in her belly.

After hearing essentially the same words again—go back to Germany now, go where the money is, take it and run—I drove home from LA with a plan.

I told Dad what she had said, and he thought that was good advice. My dad, who was raised by parents who had experienced the Great Depression, thought that if I could just make some money in this business, it would give me more security in my life. So he encouraged me to get some rest, get some sun, gain a little weight, and go back to Europe.

Over a long spaghetti dinner, while my brother used fresh bread to lap up the delicious sauce I cooked for him, he convinced me to not let myself get stuck in studios; to bring my backpack and hiking boots this time; to see places, do the business on my own terms.

Then, when the time was right, I would take the cash and run.

So after Christmas, I did.

"Be perfect for him," Giovanna, the show booker at Fashion, said to me. It was January; I was back and on my way to do the fittings for the Armani spring shows.

"What do you mean, 'Be perfect'?" I asked bitingly, turning and glaring at her. She was a snob. She had trained Tina and me to do the runway; she marketed us and got us as many show bookings as possible. But she did not care a lick about us as people. We were commodities to be bought and sold.

Her word in the fashion industry meant business. If she sold a model to someone like Giorgio Armani, that model had better deliver. The models are the product, and she only profits from them being...perfect.

"*I mean be perfect for him!*" she yelled at me as she smashed her thick brown cigarette into the ashtray. "*This is a very important job for you!*"

"Yeah, sure, I'll be perfect," I heckled under my breath as I walked past her office, out of the agency, and back onto the cobblestone street. She must have thought I didn't hear her. But I did. I heard her, and I knew exactly what it meant.

I returned to Italy without Bosquo. Mom convinced me at four o'clock in the morning, before my flight, that she would be better there at home and that I would have more freedom to travel without her. I cried when I let her go; she had become my companion.

 We don't want to be forgotten. We don't want to be cast aside. We don't want to be *unwanted.*

When I had her, I slowed down a little. I walked through the parks. That's how I learned to speak Italian: talking to old ladies in the parks. When I had her, I didn't worry so much about racing from place to place; sometimes I even skipped a casting.

Having her made me stop to eat. She had to eat, so after a long day, I came home and ate with her. At night, she would lick my cold hands and, as I wove my fingers through her fur, I would begin to thaw. She would cuddle up in my lap and look at me with adoring eyes even if I had pimples that were red and glaring.

"Be perfect." What appropriate words.

Well, guess what? I wasn't perfect.

All morning I worked with some other models while a photographer snapped pictures of us on the runway. Midday, Giorgio came out to watch us work. When it was my turn, I walked down the ramp and his gaze fell on me. He cocked his head to the side and looked at me funny. Stopping the shoot, he stepped on the stage, tugged at my skirt and stood back, perplexed.

As he studied me, my heart raced. Would he see what had become of me since the last show? Would he reject me because my body had been so hungry? Would he turn me away because the starvation had ravaged my hormones and marred my skin? Would he accept me like this?

Gently, he tugged at the fabric of my skirt, straightening the way it fell at the hem. Suddenly I remembered Momma's home cooking. *"Eat, eat, eat! You're too skinny!"* she had said when I was home, handing me a plate of chicken, potatoes, and vegetables. I pictured Christmas dinner where I had eaten heartily for the first time in months—I had gained about four pounds.

The clothes must not have hung the same on me anymore.

Then, with a flick of his hand, the designer descended the stage and began speaking with the stylist. She came over to me, took my hand, and politely led me off the stage. She took me backstage, removed my outfit, and walked away.

I stood in my underwear, shivering, feeling swallowed by the cavernous dressing room, waiting to be told what to do next. It was so embarrassing. I didn't know if they wanted to try a different outfit or send me home. Finally Matteo sent someone over to tell me I was finished for the day.

When I returned to the agency, I found out that not only did I lose all of Armani's jobs, but also I had lost *all* of my jobs.

My chart had gone mysteriously blank. If Armani didn't want me, then no one wanted me. I wasn't perfect for them anymore. I wasn't *wanted.* The bookers wouldn't even look at me.

Of course, this is the *business*. It is nothing negative about Armani or Fashion. It is the way it is. Models come and go, just as athletes come and go. You get a job; you lose a job. As Damien told me once, "One day you are the 'top.' The next, you are not. It can be snatched from you *in an instant*."

Nevertheless, there was *something* about it, something that hurt that little girl inside of me that wanted to be perfect for everyone else.

Sometimes we just cannot be all that other people want us to be.

~

"Prove yourself," I whispered as I knelt in the back pew of the little church that I passed on my morning runs. "If you hear me…if you are real…then show yourself." The sun was streaming through the stained glass windows, creating rainbows of light on the wood flooring of the aisle leading to the cross up front. The wood was old and worn from the soles of so many shoes.

I needed a miracle.

With no more jobs left on the docket, Giovanna decided to send me to Rome. She said I could do some lower-tiered shows for the Roman designers. Hoping to work a little then see some sights, I packed my big green backpack and made plans to check into a hostel afterward.

But when I arrived at the Roman train station, my backpack was stolen. A steward tried to help me find it, but it was nowhere in sight.

Frustrated and mad, I walked to the police station, my memory itemizing all of my belongings. My portfolio, passport, and money were in the bag that I still had on me; my backpack had contained my clothes, boots, scarves, gloves, sweaters and…

"Oh, no, my journal was in there! It has everything in it!" I said to myself. "Everything about me, my whole story, everything…" Tears rushed to my eyes.

Once again I found myself praying: "I don't really believe in you, God. But if you can hear me, I'll tell you: I don't care about the material things; I don't even care about the success. Whoever took that backpack can have it. You can take everything else from me…but not my journal!

"Please, please don't let everything written in there just get thrown away. It is my *heart* on the pages! At least let someone find it who can read English, so at least *someone* knows all I've been through!"

I was still brushing the tears away when a white, bulbous cab picked me up and whizzed me away to my castings.

~~

"Where's your backpack?" an Asian girl standing next to me on the bus asked. On my way from Rome back to Milan, I stopped at a hill town called Siena. Set like a tiger's eye in the emerald hillside of Tuscany, Siena has an American university that I wanted to see before I moved to Munich. I was secretly wondering if I could slip out of modeling and back into school, where I always felt best.

"My backpack?" I repeated, surprised this stranger even noticed. "Oh, it was stolen."

"So you're traveling without a backpack?"

I knew it was crazy to travel with only the clothes on my back, but I didn't care. I wanted to see some beauty more than I wanted my things. But it was January and the freezing cold eventually got to me. I finally gave in and bought gloves and a sweater.

That night I drank two beers by myself in the room and fell asleep in my clothes.

The next morning, the Asian girl—she had introduced herself as Kim—was still around, so she and I walked into town together. We wandered through the sienna-brown brick village and stop midday to have lunch. Afterward, we sat down in the *piazza*, the center square of town, which was actually a giant oval where they held horse races in the summer. The Tuscan sun, unusually warm that day, lit up the bricks with a golden hue.

Kim told me that she had been traveling by herself for seven months. Originally from New Zealand, she planned to be gone for a year before returning home. I wished her some serious luck—I knew how hard it was to be on your own in this world.

She seemed surprised. "Oh, I'm protected," she said, shrugging her shoulders. "I have nothing to worry about."

"What do you mean, 'protected'?" I asked. Did she have some kind of force field that I didn't know about?

She told me she had the Holy Spirit.

As a crew of black crows pecked at the crumbs in the square in front of us, I told her that I didn't believe in "all that stuff." So she asked me what I *did* believe—a very good question.

I explained that I had read a lot of books about Buddhism, Zen meditation, the tarot, yoga...and that I believed in a greater force out there, but maybe not exactly the One she was talking about.

"Oh, really?" she asked, looking me straight in the eyes. Her gaze hit me like a laser beam. "And how are you doing, out here, on your own? *How is your life going?*"

> ## A Word About Tarot Cards
>
> I do not support or advise anyone to use tarot cards in any way. I now fully understand how the tarot and other spiritual devices look very innocent, but are really sorcery and not of God. In fact, they can be a very dangerous way to tamper with the spiritual realm.

At first I said I was fine, but she didn't buy it. It must have been written in the wells of my eyes. I wasn't about to tell her how hard I had worked to build a career as a model in Milan, and that I felt as if I had crashed and burned.

"I feel like there is this black cloud around my head," I said, finally coming clean. "I used to be so vibrant and energetic, and now I feel so weak and tired. I have these sores on my face that won't go away. I don't know what is wrong with me anymore. I have lost so much weight. And even though I have gained some back, it's not enough." Nearly every designer in Rome, except one, had turned me away for being too thin.

Kim looked down at my bone-thin legs through my pants. "You can't have gained much," she said frankly. Her eyes brimming with compassion, she asked, "Jennifer, do you pray?"

"Sometimes, yeah, I do."

"Who do you pray to?"

"I don't know," I answered, realizing for the first time that I had no idea who I prayed to. Then I said, "Maybe it's to angels. You know, Gabriel and Raphael are the angels over people who travel." (Something I had learned from my tarot deck.)

She explained that when I pray, I should go through Jesus. I told her I didn't believe in Christianity—the whole institutionalized, religion thing. I knew some people back home who said they were Christians and their lives seemed more messed up than mine. So ever since I was a kid, I hadn't believed in "all that."

She asked me if I had ever read the Bible, and I told her no, but that I would like to.

"You know, if you want to get better," she said, "then you should ask Jesus to heal you."

I told her I'd remember that, but to be honest, I didn't think I was quite ready for it.

As the sun fell behind the clock tower that overlooked the *piazza*, Kim and I walked along the narrow, winding alleys. As is common in little Italian villages, we came upon a little church. At its entrance was a statue of what I would imagine Mary Magdalene to look like, wearing a sweeping robe and looking up at the sky in hopeful ecstasy. We decided to go in.

I loved visiting European churches. Inside, the history of mankind— and of God—is illustrated in stained glass and paintings. They are like museums.

But this church was different. It was small and empty, with nothing on the walls. There was only Jesus on the cross at the altar. He was not hanging and beaten, his body broken and gilded in gold as I have seen so many times. No, he was rising. His palms were up and his head was tilted to the side. He seemed to be welcoming us.

Kim asked me if I would like to pray with her, so I did.

We knelt. "Holy Spirit," she said, "come over Jennifer...watch over her..."

I had been so cold, continuously *freezing*. But at that moment a surge of warmth came over my back, like a hug. It was as though an eagle's wings swooped down and embraced me from behind. It was so overwhelming that all I could do was shake and tremble and cry.

When the sun finally dipped behind the hills, and Kim and I went our separate ways, she asked if it would be all right if she kept praying for me.

"Oh, sure," I said. "Why not? It can't hurt, right?"

FROM MY WORLD TO YOURS

The perfect dream for all of us is that, amidst the billions of people in the world, there will be *someone* who will stick by our side. The perfect dream is one of companionship that doesn't get up and walk out on us.

After Damien made me feel so guilty for taking Bosquo from the mountains, I tried to take her back. I returned to Como and attempted to give her to a family. I thought she would be happier with little children to play with than she would be with a lonely soul like me. But no matter how much the children called her name and tried to get her to follow them, she would not leave my side. Unleashed, she planted herself next to my hiking boots and didn't budge.

Many think that money and success are the perfect dream, but they are not. Deep inside we want someone who won't leave us for any reason or excuse. We want someone whose love is not based on our performance. We want to know that if everything unravels, we will have someone who knows our hurts and is willing to tend our wounds when invited. We don't want to be forgotten. We don't want to be cast aside. We don't want to be *unwanted*.

In the end, Damien made me feel unwanted. "I hope we are still friends," I told him back in Milan after our final dinner together.

"I have enough friends, *Jenni-fair*," he responded. "I don't need people like you in my life."

We parted because I would not bow to what he wanted. We parted because of the acne, the thinness, the loss of "beauty" that he wanted to use to catapult me to the top, as he called it. We parted because his "love" for me was conditional. He had been my manager, yes, but we had also built a close friendship, a sort of father-daughter relationship—or so I thought.

His rejection confused me. After all the rejection the average model receives, you would think it wouldn't have meant much. But it did. I thought I had found someone who was going to protect me. He certainly led me to believe he would—taking my career under his wing, going on and on about how special I was, always wanting me "at his table." But he didn't really care about me, because, when I was hurting, he withdrew his hand.

Since my own father wasn't there to hear me and look over me, it was natural for me to look for someone to take his place. But Damien discarded me. If I didn't feel disposable already, he made sure I realized that I was.

The wise teacher Beth Moore calls this a "hand withheld." When the hand of protection and security is withheld from us, it creates what she calls an "empty place." Money and success cannot fill the empty place. Men cannot fill the empty place. The longing can only be filled by God.

～ა

My pockets were stuffed with big, fat rolls of money. I had gotten up earlier that morning, walked into the agency, and cashed out. I didn't bother saying much to the bookers. I just made arrangements to go to Munich and work from there.

The Italians gave me quick kisses on each cheek, asking, as if they cared, "You will come back, won't you, *Jenni-fair?*"

"Oh, yes, I'll be back," I assured them.

One of them reminded me to return for the party to celebrate the launch of Damien's new magazine: "The directors of all the major fashion magazines will be there…*Harper's Bazaar, Vogue, Marie Claire.* You know it will be a slap in Damien's face if you do not show up. You must come back!" Damien had sworn the magazine cover would make my career skyrocket.

So I told the agency that I would be back. But as I hunkered down in the plastic chair on the train to Munich, patting the wads of money in my pockets, I closed my eyes and remembered what Damien told me: "Every good model knows when it's time to fly. So if you are going to fly, fly now, fly fast."

I knew some people suspected that my leaving Milan was about *running from something*. But, at that point, I didn't care what anyone thought anymore. I *was* running. I was flying far and flying as fast as I could.

Deep down, I knew the money would not satisfy. I knew that only love would fill me. But I had this crazy belief that money would buy me the freedom I was looking for, to leave the business and "do" life the way *I* wanted to do it.

Dad had told me that money would bring me freedom to do the things I wanted to do. In some ways, he was right. Without money, you cannot survive, let alone travel. There is nothing wrong with money per se. In fact, money *helps*! But money certainly does not *free* us.

"Success," as the world defines it, is related to the amount of money you make. But real success, according to Ecclesiastes, is *enjoying* the work that God has given us on Earth, *enjoying* our lives—finding satisfaction in the work we do (Eccles. 5:18–20). So although I had money in my pockets, I was failing. I was unhappy, so I really wasn't successful at all.

Today, I'm happy. I'm content. But my contentment doesn't come from money or success. My contentment comes from knowing that I have discovered God's perfect dream for my life. That's where the longing is filled for all of us.

IT'S IN THE WORD

God's perfect dream for you is threefold. First, it is that you know his love and therefore experience the peace and security of walking with him. Second, it is that he heals your broken heart, and brings beauty from the ashes of your life. Third, it is that you discover his plan and purpose for you. That is the meat and potatoes of the dream. Whether you end up with "success" or fortune on top of that, well then that's just gravy.

In Christ, there *is* a "happily ever after." In Jesus, God offers you the perfect companion, the One who will not leave your side and will love you through every situation and circumstance, good and bad.

The Holy Spirit, who is given to all who believe, is forever faithful, kind, and full of grace. As you walk through life, God's Spirit within you gives you direction and discernment. And as Kim said, God's Spirit protects you; he offers security. The Spirit of God does not always prevent you from going through trials, but he walks with you through them. Finally, his Spirit is a deposit, guaranteeing what is to come: eternal perfection—heaven—when you get to be with God all the time and actually see him with your own eyes.

God's plan was that I would realize *his* dream for my life, that I would find the way to the best escape route ever: the gate into the entrance of his heart, where *true* freedom lies.

God's perfect dream for you is simple but profound. According to Isaiah 61:1, Christ came to bind up your broken heart. It has been extraordinarily painful for me to open up the deep recesses of my heart and let the truth pour out in this book. But as I have done so, Christ has come in and healed the most painful of places within me: the loss of my innocence, the stolen sense of security and worth, the feeling that I was only "flesh," that I was never good enough, and that the perfect dream really *wasn't*, which caused misunderstandings between my family, whom I love so much, and me. Some wounds have been slow to mend.

But in the many, many broken places within my little-girl heart, God has helped me to heal, understand, and finally be free to allow the people in my life to be *human*, *imperfect*, and *fallible*. He has replaced my desire for "perfect" in others with *himself*. I now realize that only he is the perfect God who could have seen my confusion and read between the lines of my cries when I was hurting; only God could truly help me get out of it.

When I first surrendered my hopes and dreams to God, I felt rejected, alone, and unloved. But his undeniable love for me filled those empty places. Eventually, God gave me back a good relationship with my family. Then when I was ready, he gave me a husband, children, extended family, a church, and friends who love me deeply.

Talk about beauty from ashes. You can't *buy* this! You can't put a price tag on it. It's the only *perfect* that we can ever hope for—*a fulfilling life*—a life that doesn't continually drain us, but fills us up.

When I visited Siena, Italy, I had a plan—move to Munich, make money, then return to Siena to live as a student. But God had another plan. His plan was that I would realize *his* dream for my life. That I would find the way to the best escape route ever: the gate into the entrance of his heart, where *true* freedom lies. His perfect dream is that we will forever be in communion with him, forever be under the shadow of his protective wing, forever *known, seen, and loved*.

So what does he do with all this messy hurt in *your* heart? Romans 8:28 says he causes all things to work together for the good of those who love him. He will work it out…for the *good*.

Do you have a perfect dream for your life? It may not be your father's, your mother's, your sister's or your brother's dream for you. But that's all right.

Maybe you too have felt misunderstood and unheard. Maybe your dreams to others have seemed too distant, too idealistic, too practical, or maybe they are too lofty, too hopeful, or too fabulous. It doesn't matter what other people have dreamt for you.

What matters is what God's dreams are for your life. What does he want to "work out" in you? When he formed you in your mother's womb, he had all your days ordained for you (Ps. 139:16). He had a plan for your life. Jeremiah 29:11 says he *knows* the plans he has for you, "plans to prosper you and not to harm you, plans to give you hope and a future."

What could his plans be? What are the blueprints he carved out just for *you*? Ask him. Say to him, "What is your perfect dream for me, God? Show me! Work it out for me!" He loves prayers like that. They are invitations for him to show his power, his strength, and his love for you!

You can begin discovering God's perfect dream for you by looking at your gifts and talents. What are you good at? Certainly we know we are much *more* than meets the eye. Psalm 139:13 says God formed our "inward parts." He formed our flesh, but also he formed our souls. What ignites passion in you? What do you care about? What makes you feel beautiful and worthy, like you are contributing to the earth? It is the answers to these questions that can lead you to the purpose God had for your life when he first formed you.

If you are bold enough to follow God's purpose for your life, you'll end up on the ultimate adventure. He can use you to touch and change lives. To me, that is the ultimate success.

That, my friend, is the perfect dream, the only *perfect* we can ever hope to find.

"For I know the plans I have for you," declares the LORD, "*plans to prosper you and not to harm you, plans to give you hope and a future.* Then you will call upon me and come and pray to me, and *I will listen to you.* You will seek me and find me when you seek me with *all your heart.* I will be found by you," declares the LORD, "and will *bring you back from captivity.*"
—JEREMIAH 29: 11–13, EMPHASIS ADDED

And we know that *in all things God works for the good* of those who love him, who have been called according to his purpose.
—ROMANS 8:28, EMPHASIS ADDED

Then I realized that it is good and proper for a man to eat and drink, and to *find satisfaction in his toilsome labor* under the sun during the few days of life God has given him—for this is his lot. Moreover, when God gives any man *wealth and possessions*, and enables him to *enjoy them*, to accept his lot and be happy in his work, this is a gift of God.
—ECCLESIASTES 5:19–20, EMPHASIS ADDED

But *each man has his own gift from God*; one has this gift, another has that.
—1 CORINTHIANS 7:7, EMPHASIS ADDED

Chapter 7

THE PERFECT ESCAPE

Loneliness, Drugs, and Suicide

itting at the kitchen table in Munich, I watch the snow fall steadily out the window, miniature tufts of cotton swirling in a hazy fog. Most of the time, snow is magical to me; it makes me want to hunker down indoors, cuddling in front of the fire with a blanket and a book, surrounded by the people I love.

But this is not that kind of snow; this is a lonely snow. There is no chance of that magical warmth now, no hope or dream of it even, as I sit at the table alone in silence. I have no love around me, and my family is too far away to even wish for their embrace.

The tabletop before me is a scattered array of rolling tobacco, a half-burnt block of hash, used matches, the old remains of a cup of tea, and a few empty beer bottles. My eyes are half-open and my heart is slammed shut. I am alone. Not the kind of alone that you enjoy, not a refreshing solitude, but an aloneness that has wrapped itself around me like a huge black cloak. I feel so insignificant inside of it—cut off from life outside, shrunken to the feeling that I am too small for the world's meanness, too weak for its strength, too meager to fight the battles it will take to get back out there and live beautifully again.

It seems to happen all at once, like a landslide. I've fought my way to the top, having been cut and bruised along the way, but I've made it. But now, I begin slipping and clawing for a foothold. I am falling, and the rocks and boulders start rushing so fast they carry me away in their current.

The whirlwind of dust and pebbles, and then huge boulders, cascading around me sweeps me away in a violent avalanche. It is a wicked, ruthless, unforgiving fall. When I land at the bottom of the mountain, I am battered and beaten. I feel broken all over.

I've ignored the gaping hole in my heart for as long as I can. But the hole is beginning to scream at me. The hollow-ness I saw backstage refuses to let me be, no matter how I avoid it. It invades me in nightmares, calling to me in the middle of the night. It holds me down in the mornings when I want to get up but can't. I cannot not get away from it, no matter how much designer clothing and jewelry I wear; it hunts me down until finally it has me pinned.

What We're Really Longing For

Escape: *to get away as by flight; to break free from confinement; to evade or avoid something undesirable; to seek relief from reality*

We all have times when we want to *run away*. We want to *fly* and to *break free*. But in life, the more we try to run from the hole in our hearts, the bigger it gets. Geographically, we think that if we relocate, it will be better. Physically, we think that if we take something that dulls the pain, it will be better.

To escape is to seek relief from reality. But life is tricky; most of the things the world promises will bring relief are only temporary solutions. In the long term, they do not deliver.

When the cab driver dropped me off at 66 *Rosenheimerstrasse*, the address of my new apartment building in Munich, I immediately felt the alienation of not knowing a soul in the entire country.

I was relieved to be out of Milan, though: out of the clutches of Damien and his son; away from the suffocating traffic, smog, and chaos that were choking the life out of me. It was better to be in Munich, where I'd heard there were parks and trees and clean air—though it was a shame to be there without my little dog Bosquo.

There was one thing for sure; if I did need anyone, I had no intention of calling the agency in Hamburg, not after what had happened with the Miami job. They must have heard that the young, pretty seventeen-year-old girl who was such a success a few years ago had disintegrated into a—as that photographer called me—*depressed, insecure, anorexic mess with acne.* Thank goodness my Munich agency hadn't heard *his* view of their new model coming to town.

I dragged my suitcases up four flights of stairs, fiddled with three locks, and swung the door open to view my new dwelling. The apartment had cold, blond hardwood floors that led down a short hallway that branched off into two bedrooms, a kitchen, and a bath. At first it seemed as if no one lived there. I had been told that I had a roommate—a lingerie model. She was away on some exotic island for a two-week job and was due to come back that weekend.

I walked back and forth between the two bedrooms, trying to figure out which one was hers. All the cupboards and shelves in both rooms were empty and the hall closet was locked. Even the cabinets in the kitchen were bare. Finally I settled on the room near the bathroom, guessing it was mine. A single twin mattress with two wool blankets lay on the floor opposite a window, the light of which streamed into the room and cast a golden hue over the bed. I figured that window would be my saving grace.

All week long I worked and went to castings—at least eight a day in order to meet all the clients and photographers in the city. As in Paris and Milan, I spent just as much time underground as I did aboveground. But in Munich, the people in the metro looked even *more* miserable, something I didn't think was possible. They appeared as if they were just bearing the misery of another day on Earth as they stared out the windows with a cold, distant gaze, their bodies passively jiggling with the pulse of the train.

If I did make eye contact with a man or woman on the street or metro, in return I received a cold, hard look as they quickly averted their eyes. So, on the trains I too looked out the window, beyond my reflection, daydreaming about home or trying to think of nothing at all.

One time, in a sudden burst of energy, some children jumped on board, laughing and joking, giggling under their breath about some secret they shared. Their bright faces reminded me of children in the metros of Milan, standing arm-in-arm in their school uniforms, filling the car with the sounds of their boisterous laughter. Their jubilant spirits were in such sharp contrast to the dead souls of the old men who staunchly held their newspapers in front of their faces, refusing to engage in conversations or even make eye contact. In all seriousness, I began to wonder if I would travel the whole world and find that children were the only ones who laughed.

 You try *anything* to escape the pain. But, eventually, you cannot escape it because it follows you. You cannot ignore it because it is too big. It gets in the way of everything.

Just as I had in so many cities, I walked all over Munich, meeting with men who looked at me; asked me to turn around, walk, smile for the camera, try on this bathing suit or that fur coat; and sent me away without speaking any more of my language than was required. The agency wasn't much better—even though this one was run by women rather than men. One lady was warm to me when I came in. She always asked how things were going, but she was not there full-time.

The rest of the staff simply gave me instructions on where to go and when to be there, nothing more. Never a "How are you?" or "How was your day?" Just do this and do that, be here and go there. I didn't know what it was that made those people so closed, but I couldn't imagine that I would ever fit in there. Each day as I walked the icy sidewalk that led to my apartment, I questioned what on earth I was doing in that place.

In the evenings I came home to nothing. There was only dark, empty, cold silence, except for the periodic huff of the water heater. I walked from room to room, my thick wool socks scratching the floorboards. There was no one to talk to, no TV to watch, no music to listen to, no one to call.

I bought myself a block of Moroccan hash from a model at a casting and rolled my cigarettes with it. It was the strangest thing, but I began reading Anne Rice's *Lestat*, a novel about communities of vampires that live and feed off people in the undergrounds of cities. At night after work, sometimes I got high, sometimes I drank, sometimes I read or wrote in a half-finished journal from childhood that I had grabbed from home.

But sometimes I painted. I loved the feel of the stroke of the brush—it was so soothing. The only canvas I had was one Damien had given me in Italy. It had started out beautiful, a bright blue sky over a sapphire sea, but I destroyed the beauty by painting over it with a mire of fiery flames. After that, I painted old water bottles for something to do. Covering them with a wet, sandy paste, I let them dry overnight, and then painted them in blue swirls like the Pacific.

I made a couple thousand dollars a day wearing tacky warm-up suits and heavy makeup for cheap catalogs. I knew on the train to Munich that the money wouldn't make me happy, but what else was I going to do? Nina and I had made a plan: make as much money as I could—and Germany was the place to do it; milk the business for all it was worth—after all, it had milked *me* for all *I* was worth.

~~❧~~

It was Valentine's Day, and I had a job posing as a bride. The dresses were made of cheap satin and tasteless ruffles that I could hardly stand to put on; they were nothing like the Italian gowns crafted of rare silk and delicate chiffon, cut in exquisite lines that formed to my body.

Here, everything felt *cheap* to me, but I was being paid three times as much, and it seemed horrible to complain.

Back in Milan, when I told Damien that I was questioning whether to model anymore, he had looked at me with disdain. "You spit on the very plate that feeds you," he scowled. "It is a terrible thing to do."

So, cheap satin or not, I closed my eyes and tried to hide my cringes as the makeup artist painted layers and layers of makeup over the dark circles under my eyes and poked at my pimples with his dirty makeup brush, endlessly trying to mask them with cover-up.

When I saw my reflection in the mirror—so made-up, so fake, so artificial and *not me*—I pretended like I didn't hate what I saw. But I did. I hated it. I hated myself for not being true to who I was and for not even *knowing* who I was underneath all the layers. I felt uglier than I had in my entire life. And they were going to use these pictures of me in their magazine? Why?

It reminded me of a passage from *Martin Eden*: "Beauty hurts you. It is an everlasting pain in you, a wound that does not heal, a knife of flame. Why should you palter with magazines? Let beauty be your end. Why should you mint beauty into gold?"[1]

In front of the camera, I had to do my job, so I pretended to be a joyous bride—totally in love with a guy in a tuxedo who looked exactly like a Ken doll. He held a plastic rose in his teeth that was as artificial as he was. His breath revolted me. All I could think was, "This is such a joke. I could never marry someone as plastic as you."

The makeup artist came over and stuffed some shoulder pads down the front of my dress to make my breasts look bigger, telling me, in no uncertain terms, to look happy. I didn't want these people to dress me up like a doll anymore; I didn't want them touching my face and tugging at my hair, nipping and tucking at the clothes I wore like I was some sort of mannequin. I wanted to be left alone.

The shoot ended midday, and I couldn't get home fast enough to wash off the makeup. From the metro stop, I ran through the snow, up the stairs, through the door of my apartment, and straight to the sink. Splashing hot, soapy water on my face, I scrubbed and scrubbed until my skin was red and raw. I put on my sweats, took a few drags off a leftover joint, and crawled into bed. Even though it was still daylight, I pulled the covers over my head.

I didn't even want to be here anymore. "Besides," I thought, "what's the point? I've lost my beauty."

"*La vita è bella,*" the man on the street had told me. Life is beautiful.

But what did that mean?

My mind drifted back to a recent interview. "Her legs are beautiful," the booker had said to the client, pointing at a picture in my portfolio. I was seventeen in the picture, my skin was smooth and supple. But when I went to the interview, the client noticed my bruises and scars and sent me away.

"They aren't beautiful anymore," the photographer said to the booker, and sent me on my way.

To me, beauty was expendable; it was here one day and gone the next. It was an everlasting pain in me; it was a wound that wouldn't heal; it was a knife of flame.

I nestled even further under the covers, read a few more pages of my vampire novel, and drifted off to sleep.

～⁓

I dreamt I was falling, turning, twisting, clawing, kicking, fighting, spinning in circles of flashing light that came from all angles of a black trajectory. There seemed no end to my descent, and I began to cry, but the storm spewed back my tears in vicious rain. A tumultuous wind forced me through the chute of an endless tunnel…I screamed, and a cacophony of voices answered me, all confused, borne of the hollow dark.

"You have bad skin because you do not eat meat!" A fat man's face laughed and danced across the trajectory.

Marcello poked his head from the space, his hair shining like an angel's. "Are you tired, *Jenni-fair*? You should take some sun!" His voice echoed through the tortuous tube in which I traveled.

Eyes like black fortune-teller's balls bobbed at me. Lasers shot at me, penetrating my sores. Damien grinned, his teeth shining in the blue-black night.

I heard the phone ring, but I couldn't get to it. I couldn't open my eyes and break through the dream. I was falling and spinning through the emptiness. Voices flew at me, screaming and calling from every edge of the world:

"Beautiful, beautiful! Let me see her pictures! Try this on! I am sorry the shoes don't fit, but you must wear them. Smile with your eyes, not your mouth. Be natural! Can you be sexy? I need you to be romantic. Change her lips; make them fuller; make them darker! Is that a bruise? She has a pimple. What did you do, eat a bunch of chocolate? You should take better care of your skin. Pretend you are in love! Be serious, *Jenni-fair*. Your hair, it is like an angel's; I love it! Can you make your hair straight? Your eyes are so blue; are they real? Watch her eat—like a bird—how delicate she is! Eat this! Eat that! Eat more! Eat less! Have dinner with me; come to bed with me; get high with me! Open your robe; pull up your dress; I must see your breasts; I must see your thighs. We can't show her legs. The pictures are beautiful. The pictures are terrible. The client loved you! The client hated you! *Bella! Bella!*"

Another shrill ring of the telephone drove me from the bed. I shuffled out to the phone in the hallway and picked it up.

It was the agency. The booker's voice was as far away as home. "*Jenni-fur*, you have an appointment in forty-five minutes at the Madison Hotel. It is number twenty-eight in your book. You will see Hans, a very important photographer. The pay is two thousand marks."

"Uh-huh," I muttered, drowning out her voice. I heard a click, and the phone slipped from my hand and tumbled to the floor.

"No!" I screamed. "I can't do this anymore! If they send me on one more casting to meet one more jerk, I will die!" I turned and looked down the hallway, into the bathroom mirror. My face was a bruised, punctured peach. I moved closer to my reflection and saw that the shadows around my eyes had become trenches. There was almost no spark of life left in them, nothing except a faint light buried beneath layers of makeup and hairdos and pictures and eyes of people. The corners of my mouth were pulling, pulling me down.

"I don't want to live my life like this," I cried, my eyes filling with tears. I slid to the ground, curling into a ball, sobbing. It was as if someone had taken my heart and wrung it out like a rag.

I crawled to the kitchen and pulled myself up at the stove. Shaking, I lit a match and fired up the burners. I grabbed the roach from last night's joint off the shelf, held it up to the flame, and my chipped red nails caught fire. I let them become the lighter as I sucked the last bit of juice out of the roach.

I filled one large and one small pot with water, placed them on the flame to boil, and sat down at the meager wooden table, cluttered with the leftovers of last night's overindulgence: cigarettes, hash, rolling papers, and beer. "Where is that witch I live with anyway?" I thought. "Is misery in company more tolerable?"

I drifted off, remembering the only time I ever saw my roommate. She had dark skin, cropped brown hair, and hazel eyes that must have been quite exotic-looking for the lingerie catalogs. But she had a repugnant ugliness about her that must not have been detectable on film. I had been alone in Munich for about ten days when she came home for just one night. Looking forward to meeting her, I shopped for dinner, planning to make her my spaghetti and hoping that we would eat together and get to know each other a bit.

 It is not where you are; it is *whom* you run to that counts.

As soon as she got home, she closed herself off in her room, talking on the phone for nearly an hour. Hoping that she would come out, I put the sauce on the stove and let it simmer while I sat down at the kitchen table and read.

When she did emerge, it was only to say that a blanket was missing from her couch. I quickly explained that I had used it for yoga, apologized, and immediately went to get it from my room.

When I came back, she grabbed it out of my hands. "That's why I lock everything up in the closet," she snapped. "You models come in here and act like this is your home and take whatever you want! I got so sick and tired of you stealing my stuff that I finally had to lock everything away every time I go."

"Oh, I—I would never steal..." I stuttered in return.

"Well, you shouldn't have used the blanket without my permission. But I've had much worse—girls wear my clothes, take off with my makeup; it's crazy. It's not like this is your home! You are *visitors*, and you people just don't understand that!"

Feebly, I told her I was really sorry and had made some spaghetti for us for dinner if she wanted some. But she rudely turned it down, heating up a frozen box of her own pasta, taking it to her room, and shutting herself in for the rest of the night. When I woke up the next morning, she was gone, off on a weeklong trip.

"Mom, this is not my home," I tried to explain to her on the phone the next day. "It's like I'm a visitor here; nothing is mine." I tried to tell her and Dad that I still wanted to quit, I didn't want to keep going, but they couldn't understand. I guess they didn't believe in quitting.

On top of it all, they told me my Grandma Betty, my dad's mother, was sick. She had had osteoporosis for a while, but apparently her spine was now collapsing. And my little Bosquo had been attacked by a pack of coyotes. She survived, but she was not well.

Before we got off the phone, Dad reminded me that Nina and I decided I would stick it out for another year. "I know, Dad, but I can't. I don't want to."

We ended up agreeing that I would "hang in there" for at least a few more months.

~~~

I was stirred out of my thoughts by the bubbles in the small pot roaring on the stove. I took some herbs from a worn paper sack and poured them into the boiling water. The man at the herb store had promised me that if I drank this tea three times a day, I would get my period. But it had already been a few weeks and nothing had happened—I hadn't menstruated in over six months, and I was sick of this tea.

I poured myself a cup anyway and sat down at the table, lighting a candle stuck into the one water bottle I had painted red. Ghosts of steam rose from the mug. The water heater made its obnoxious huff. My head pounded as if there were a little man inside my brain with a miniature hammer, tapping away at the final nail that would seal my coffin. The crimson swirls on the bottle looked like blood in the shadows. I looked out at the falling snow and missed having someone in my life who loved me.

The tea tasted bitter, and I soon tired of it. I got up, rummaged through my backpack for coins, put them in my coat pocket, piled on the layers—sweater, boots, scarf, coat, hat, gloves—and walked out the door, leaving the big pot steaming on the stove.

I hurried down the stairs and outside into the cold, snowflakes flying into my already burning eyes. Through the haze, a red light shone in the distance, and I headed straight toward it. I walked into a smoky bar and struggled in my limited German to order two beers to go. "After all," I thought, "it seems silly to buy just one."

The old men hunched at the counter turned and looked at me with the same icy stare I saw every day on the street and in the metro. The barmaid gave me the extra-tall beers; I paid her and walked back to the apartment. Once inside, I peeled off the layers of clothing, popped open one bottle, downed some of the beer, and threw some spaghetti in the boiling pot.

I set the table for two, poured two beers, prepared two bowls of spaghetti, and sat with my journal, pretending to make dinner conversation with someone—someone who saw me as I was at that moment, someone who knew me in that awful state and loved me anyway, the lover of my soul.

But he did not exist.

I was surrounded by darkness except for the candle. I watched the flame sway and stared out the window at the snowy world.

In angry rebellion to the world of calories, I downed both beers and ate both bowls of spaghetti until my stomach was painfully bloated. In self-disgust, I smoked another joint, inhaling in long drags. My head hurt. My mouth and eyes hurt. My heart hurt. I walked to the window and pried it open, leaning my head out to feel the frozen crystals landing on my face.

"God..." I muttered, but I knew no God who saw me.

Wishing I could throw up but knowing I could never bring myself to, I walked to the bathroom, put the plug in the tub, and shoved on the hot water. Stripping naked, I walked around the house and closed all the doors. Vapors rose from the tub, fogging the mirror. I placed the red bottle on the edge of the tub, the candle's flame creating shadowy spirits that danced on the tiles. Dipping my toe in the water, I could feel that it burned, but I stepped in anyway and let my feet scald. It was like I *wanted* to burn myself.

As I lowered myself in, my goose pimples stung. Splashing hot water over my puffy, sore face, I felt like an old woman who had seen too much. I ran my hands along my legs, disgusted to see that they were bony and bruised. My hands were a sickly mint green, and their sores looked purple under the water.

I was shivering and scared, but I knew what I was going to do. Numb, I turned on my belly, stretched my limbs to the corners of the tub, and dunked my head under. It was blistering hot against my face. My cheeks and eyes bulged, and I felt like my skin was about to burst.

A string of memories flashed across my mind. I was a little girl, picking strawberries in Grandma Betty's strawberry patch. Then I was at home in our backyard, playing on a vast bank of daisies. I swung on the swing; I dug in the sandbox; I sat atop our playhouse and sailed round the world. Greg chased me over the field of daisies, my pinafore dress rippling in the wind. I made cherry pies sitting on the kitchen counter with Mom; picked fruit from the orchard with Dad. I learned to ride a bike in the cul-de-sac; I made sand castles on the shore; I was beautiful then...pure.

The memories stopped. My eyes were bulging against my eyelids, and I wanted to breathe, but I was determined to keep my head down as long as I could. I pressed my hands and feet harder against the porcelain tub, determined to not let them slip, yet knowing I probably couldn't do this. I still wanted to try.

"Who would care right now if I died? Would anyone? No one on *this* continent!" I reasoned, straining to keep myself down and trying not to cry under the water.

Then I thought of Greg, Mom, Dad, Trish…and a sob broke loose. I gasped in the water and it went down my windpipe. I shot up out of the water like a geyser, choking, spitting, and gasping for air.

FROM MY WORLD TO YOURS

Drugs play tricks on you. They tell you, as do many other things in life—food, sex, money, possessions—if you just keep on getting as much of them as you can, they will eventually fill the void inside you. The strange thing is, you take drugs to *avoid* facing the emptiness and you take them to *fill* it at the same time.

Drugs—which I began doing in college, not in the modeling industry—started out as just a way of having fun, getting high, partying. It seemed like simple, normal experimentation. In college there was always access to Ecstasy, acid, mushrooms, pot, heroin, coke, nitrous— you name it. It wasn't only one class or social group who used them; if the rich kids weren't doing it in the smelly frat houses, then the homeless crack addicts were doing it on the sidewalk around the corner.

If you use drugs "only recreationally," as I did, then you might think, "What's the big deal? I'm just having fun, copping a buzz, getting high. It's not like I'm doing anything different than the rest of my peers! It's not like I'm shooting up! It's not like I'm *addicted*!" Well, I've got news for you: an addict, an alcoholic, a pothead, a doper, a tripper, and a "recreational" user all have something in common. They all had a first time. They were able to tell themselves the same things you are thinking right now. But for many, it didn't stop there. They went from recreational use to addiction to try to escape that which is within.

Many people drink, take drugs, overeat, diet or exercise excessively, overspend, even travel incessantly in an attempt to run from their lives, to numb the pain. For these people, lighting up that joint, pouring the drink, fixing the needle, or whipping out the credit card is, in essence, saying, "Today I am not going to feel the pain. I am not going to feel the emptiness, the loneliness, the sadness, or the loss. Instead, I will take this. I will buy that. I will go there, and it will make me feel better or feel nothing, and I won't have to face this gaping hole in my heart today."

But when they wake up the next day, the buzz has worn off, the credit card bills come due, and the pain is worse. It is wider. It is deeper. So they need *more* to fill it up. They need more drugs, more alcohol, more stuff…more, more, more.

They try food. They try sex. They try sleeping. They try hiding under the blankets. They try running away. They try *anything* to escape the pain. But, eventually, they cannot escape it because it follows them. They cannot ignore it because it is too big. It gets in the way of everything that really matters—family, friends, health, career, *life.*

For me, the drugs went from being "recreational" to being what I thought was my perfect escape. They became my way to fly away, to avoid the undesirable, to seek some relief from reality. I felt confined, and I wanted to break free.

Drugs, in this generation, are touted as a way to expand your mind, to broaden your horizons, to see things in a new light. At times it may seem as though they accomplish this in one way or another. But remember, after they light you up, they always burn you out. And then they just become a way to dull the truth, to blur reality, to avoid facing those things in your life that you don't want to face.

When I lived in Milan and was involved in an unhealthy relationship, hash served as a veil between the longings of my little-girl heart and the realization that my life had become just about as depressing as it could be. I'll refrain from sharing the details, but it's enough to say that I was with someone who had abused me, someone whom I did not love, and drugs became a way to avoid those truths, to bury them and not have to deal with them.

If you turn to drugs to find relief from reality, the relief is only temporary. It's never life changing. It doesn't permanently transform you from the inside out.

Drugs or any other temporary relief can do nothing for the sin in your heart, your broken dreams, or the ways that loved ones have hurt or betrayed you. Drugs and alcohol cannot heal you. In many ways, they only hurt you more, to the point that healing and real, lasting freedom from the vise grip they put on your life become almost impossible to imagine.

That which you seek within your own self to set you free from confinement actually ends up firmly holding you there.

IT'S IN THE WORD

Today, God has become my great escape. I am not saying I'm never tempted to go back to those old ways. Of course I am. Oh, a glass of wine—or three—might loosen me up and help me relax. A little pot won't hurt, right?

Of course I've fallen since I first asked Jesus Christ to come in my heart! Who hasn't?

But with those few falls, God has picked me up and given me a better understanding about sin and consequences, escape routes and real refuges, than I ever had before. Our brokenness gives him a chance to put us back together as he sees fit; it gives us some teachable moments when we can learn what it truly means to walk *free* in Christ.

I will never say that I have been or that I am a perfect Christian. That just does *not* exist. And that label can also become a mask we wear to make ourselves look good.

That which you seek within your own self to set you free from confinement actually ends up firmly holding you there.

Yuck, I hate masks—God hates masks! Personally, I've had enough of them!

But healing is possible. Relief is possible. Freedom is possible.

God wants, more than anything, to be your rock of refuge, the place you desperately run to with your hurts, disappointing realities, and heartbreaking relationships. Over and over and over again in his Word, God invites you to come to him and let him be your refuge, your hiding place from the storm. He wants to hold you in the "hammock" of his everlasting arms. Let him bring you the peace you so desire. Because he can!

That pipe cannot; that needle cannot; that drink cannot; those pills cannot. But God can!

He made the earth, he made every star in the sky, and he made you. God loves you. He loved you enough to give his Son, Jesus, as your ransom. Jesus bought the freedom from all your pain, hurts, and disappointments with his own suffering. He suffered and died for you. His blood makes you clean; his broken body makes you whole.

Read his Word. Instead of drugs and alcohol, it will be the medicine your soul needs.

He is God...the Almighty...the Great I AM. As Beth Moore says, he is not the "I was." He is not the "I will be." He is the "I AM." He is here, today, now. And he is calling *your* name! Can you hear him?

God weeps and longs for a relationship with you. His arms are always open; run to him. When you run to him, he will run even faster toward you. He will pick you up and hold you like the little girl you are inside, and he will make you whole again.

The Bible says God invites you to rest in the shadow of his healing wings the same way a mother bird shelters her young. Let him carry you; let him love you. If you run to him, he will accept you and love you just as you are. He will become your *perfect escape*.

When people get to the level of depression, addiction, disappointment, hurt, and unhealthy lifestyle that I reached, they usually take one of three paths:

1. They kill themselves trying to fill or escape the emptiness.
2. They hit rock bottom, call for help, and get it.
3. They live *in the loneliness*—they stay there.

I've known people who have chosen each path.

After college, a friend of mine died from heroin use. He lived in a house in Newport Beach, California, with a few college friends. I heard some of our buddies found him dead in the bathroom one morning, a needle hanging out of his arm.

We were all gambling with our lives back then—no matter what kind of drugs we were doing—and for some reason we didn't know how precious we were, or how fragile. Even our good friend's death didn't stop many people, including ones whom I loved the most, from continuing down that road.

When I met my husband, Shane, he made me feel immediately comfortable with my past because what I had been through was *peanuts* compared to what he had seen. Both of us had been *saved*—physically and spiritually—by the hand of God. That truth forged a unique and lasting understanding between us.

Shane used to be a heavy drug user; throughout his travels he witnessed many people die from overdosing. Right before his eyes, they turned blue, cold, and lifeless! Countless times he and his friends found themselves frantically putting ice on them, splashing cold water on them, and slapping them in an attempt to bring them back. Many did not make it back; they never had a chance to live life beyond all the senseless partying.

One day, Shane packed up his truck and came home—strung out, hurting, and at rock bottom. He had realized he did not want to live his life in the endless cycle of highs and lows that drugs bring. Drawing on the Christian faith instilled in him as a child, he called out for help, moved back in with his parents, and followed all their rules to get his life on track. He rededicated his life to God, and God carried him through the *brutally painful process* of getting clean. He marvels at his life today; he can't contain all the blessings.

I know a lot of people who never come out of that life. They *stay* there—they live in it. Some people never completely give up the drugs or alcohol (or whatever their addiction). They never find the source of the emptiness, so they never find the cure for it.

They live in that place where I was—at the kitchen table in Munich—trying endlessly to mask the loneliness, to numb the pain.

My heart aches most for these people because they are missing out on what Christ describes as "life to the full." He said that the enemy, the devil, "comes only to steal and destroy"—as he did to me—but Jesus came so that we "may have life, and have it to the full" (John 10:10).

The way to the "full" life is *surrender*. It is surrendering the emptiness to God and asking him to fill your heart. This is what I did—and still do—because my heart still becomes empty and dried up if I don't ask God to fill it up. How does he fill it? Through his Word, through prayer, and through spending time with and learning from other Christians.

By the time I surrendered my life to God, my heart was not only empty; it was also *broken*. The good news about God is that he will accept us even if we are broken, and he will put us back together— his way. If your heart is empty, or even broken, God can fix it. He can rebuild any broken life. And then he will fill it. It all starts with giving your life to him. God created the universe; fixing your life is not a challenge for him. No one is too far gone. If Shane and I were not too far gone, you or that someone you love is not too far gone either.

~

When I was in the bathtub in my apartment in Germany, holding myself under hot water and wishing it would all go away, I had no idea that the perfect escape route was within my grasp. God was right there with me, ready to open his arms and hold his lost and hurting little girl. I only needed to ask him to.

Are you looking for a perfect escape? Do you need a place to run where everything will be all right, where you are safe and happy? A place where that cavern in your heart is completely filled? I have traveled the world, searching for the perfect place to be, and have discovered—as Dorothy did when she clicked her heels three times and returned home from Oz—that it was available to me all along. It was right there, in my own backyard.

It's not where you are; it's *whom* you run *to* that counts.

God never tires of your needs. He never runs out of time. Because he made you, he knows better than anyone how to comfort and love you; he knows what you need. Run to him; let him become your perfect escape, your refuge in a world too cruel for our little-girl hearts.

How priceless is your *unfailing love!* Both high and low among men find *refuge in the shadow of your wings.*

—PSALM 36:7, EMPHASIS ADDED

As for God, his way is perfect; the word of the LORD is flawless. He is a *shield* for all who *take refuge in him.*

—2 SAMUEL 22:31, EMPHASIS ADDED

My soul thirsts for you, my body longs for you, in a dry and weary land where *there is no water.*

—PSALM 63:1, EMPHASIS ADDED

Come, all you who are thirsty, come to the waters; and you who have no money, come, buy and eat! Come, buy wine and milk without money and without cost. *Why spend money* on what is not bread, *and your labor on what does not satisfy?* Listen, listen to me, and eat what is good, and *your soul will delight in the richest of fare. Give ear and come to me*; hear me, that your soul may live. I will make an everlasting covenant with you, my faithful love.

—ISAIAH 55:1–3, EMPHASIS ADDED

Chapter 8

THE PERFECT PATH

The Wide and Narrow Roads

he River Isar runs cold, blue, and alive through Munich, creating the setting for many parks. I am walking along the river, strolling through the beer gardens that dot the shore; eyeing pretzels, schnitzel, and tall glasses of beer; enjoying but envying the happy couples, running children, and friendly dogs that have come to the park to savor the beautiful day. It's a Sunday afternoon, the day after I held myself under the bathwater. After tossing and turning in my bed for fourteen hours, I've dressed and chosen to go for a walk through the park, kind of the way one chooses life over death.

I come upon some girls riding horses, and I ask about them. I have always loved horses and would really like to ride. They point me to a distant part of the park, and I head in that direction but lose my way. Finally I decide to head back toward the river so I don't get stuck in the far reaches of the park after dark. Near the shore, I hear the sound of drums.

Naturally, I follow the sound, and it grows louder, and my curiosity, stronger. I walk up a steep, dirt hillside that leads to an enormous white stone gazebo perching like an eagle over the park. People are playing music, eating, talking, getting ready to enjoy the sunset over the steeple-studded horizon. As the sky fades to lavender, I sit down and enjoy a drum circle, but it dies out. So I move to another one that is just starting up.

Planting myself against the base of a pillar, I meditate on the hands that beat the drums. It feels good to enjoy the warmth of people—people who do not know me, do not speak my language, but do not size me up either. The drums dip to a lull, the sky turns deep purple, and behind me, the most melodious voice is singing; it is like the voice of an angel. I turn around to see who it is and am surprised to see a quite large, burly man with thick curly hair and huge hands.

He looks kindly down at me, rotates his guitar to the side, and reaches into a box of books. "Das Neue Testament," *he says, handing me the book.*

"No speakanse Deutsch" *is my feeble attempt to tell him I don't speak German. I take the book anyway, looking at its soft blue cover and gold title.*

"Das Neue Testament," *he repeats.* "Das New Testament?"

"Oh, this is the Bible!" *I say. Immediately, Kim comes to mind.*

I spend a little time talking to this man and his friends— they speak very little English, and the only thing I know how to say in German is, "I don't speak German." *When it grows dark and time to leave, they invite me to come to their church with them that coming Friday night. I don't know a soul in the country, and I have nothing to do on Friday night, so I think,* "Why not?"

Inside the little brick church, it is warm. People laugh. Children run here and there, playing, singing, and giggling. The people seem to really care about each other, and they seem to care about me. They even find an English version of the Good News Bible for me.

When they hand it to me, it is as if they hand me a glass of water. It is that simple. There is no deep, theological discussion, no mindful study, no political debate. It is a glass of water being handed to a very, very thirsty girl, and I take it.

And I drink, and drink, and drink, and drink.

What We're Really Longing For

A Path: *a trodden way, course or route; a way of life, conduct or thought*

The path we take in life is marked by twists and turns. Many believe there are no accidents. Some realize—usually with maturity—what humongous implications turning "right" or "left" down any given path can have on the outcome of our lives.

Certainly my first trip to Europe at seventeen changed me. That first contract was a deed that altered the course of my life; it had a far different impact on me than would have, say, an invitation to join a volleyball team. The path you take in life is so very important. Each choice, each turn, can lead to roads of desolation or freedom.

I started on the path to desolation when I began experimenting with drugs and sex. Those choices had repercussions that still exist today, no matter how clean God has made my slate. We cannot always change what is already set in motion because of a choice or decision. The choices we make, the routes we take, lead to destinations that can often not be reversed. We *cannot* go back.

But what we *can* do is jump over to a better path. Turning from darkness to light *is* possible. Like Dorothy clicking her heels and popping straight home, it really is that simple with God: click your heels—choose God—"And I'll take you home," he

says, "*home, where you belong.*" It begins with the courage
to say, "This path has led me to a dark place, and I want to
walk in the light. *Take me to the light, God.*"

"The ax is ready to cut down the trees at the roots," I read at the kitchen
table in Munich. "Every tree that does not bear good fruit will be cut
down and thrown in the fire" (Matt. 3:10, GNT).

I chuckled. Was it the hash that made my head as thick as brewing
thunderclouds? Was it the vampire novels I'd been reading night after
night? Was it the fact that a few days ago I posed as a bride during the
day and nearly killed myself hours later?

Good fruit? What good fruit was in my life? What good thing was
coming out of my life? "None," I whispered. "None."

A fruitless life is the mark of being on the wrong path. By fruit, I
mean the "love, joy, peace, patience, kindness, goodness, faithfulness,
gentleness and self-control" that the Book of Galatians refers to as the
fruit of the Spirit (Gal. 5:22–23). At the time, I did not even know what
the "fruit of the Spirit" was—I had not yet finished reading the Gospels,
so Galatians was chapters away. But in each of our hearts, we know the
meaning of "fruit"—*lasting results of our actions that make our lives meaningful.* Something to show for our lives—not a book of credentials, but
proof that our hearts are full, and from them we are contributing to the
world, offering the "fruits" of our labor to enrich those around us.

I was painting another old water bottle when I got the urge to open
that Bible again. The book was small and could fit in the palm of my
hand; its pages were thin and browned with age. Someone had taken
care to reinforce the cover by gluing a photograph of a pasture to the
front and back. The picture was of a single sheep grazing in a green
field, behind it the silhouette of an oak tree and a pale blue sky.

I flipped the book open and landed on a story about two roads—
one wide and one narrow. My head was so thick with hashish, I could
barely read. I stared at the blurry page until I got it—the wide road is
easy and crowded, but leads to nowhere; the narrow road is hard, but
leads to life (Matt. 7:13–14).

I passed my finger back and forth through the flame of a candle, creating a stripe of blackened skin. I looked around at the table scattered with a lighter, a mess of tobacco leaves, and rolling papers, and at the dark night out the window. I thought of the models, lining up in droves, vying for a job on the runway.

The wide road, I realized. *This is the wide road.*

Then I heard a voice—a voice that was audible only from within. "Throw it out," it said.

"Throw what out?" I asked aloud.

"The hash," was the response. "Throw it out so I can talk to you."

I looked down at the hash. It was my friend—the only thing that numbed me, the only thing that helped me escape. But right then I needed *life* more than I needed *it.* I wanted *life* and I wanted *fruit* more than I wanted to live in this death any longer. And somehow I knew I had to choose.

I picked up the cigarettes and the hash and walked to the bathroom. Shaking, I opened the satchel and let the broken brown clumps splatter into the toilet. I wet the tobacco under the faucet until it was sopping wet and tossed it in the trash. Pressing down on the lever, I flushed the toilet and watched my source of counterfeit "peace" swirl in diminishing circles and disappear. Pain drilled through my brow, leaving a throbbing, dull ache that pounded my eye sockets. I blew out the candle and took the vampire book with me to bed.

FROM MY WORLD TO YOURS

We are the sheep; he is the shepherd (John 10:11). When we go astray or have been astray all our lives, he calls us to come back into the sheepfold—so that we are not alone, estranged, and wandering, but instead part of a protected, loved, and cared-for community. It doesn't really matter what form the voice of the shepherd comes in; it doesn't matter how far we have gone astray or what our reasons were for wandering.

What matters is this: when God calls, do you hear his voice and do you come? (See John 10:4.)

When he says, "Come over to this path—that one is hurting you or will hurt you" (for reasons we may not even comprehend)—do we *resist* the voice of the shepherd? Or do we *come*? Only God can see down the path; only God knows the future. So when he calls to you and says, "I am the good shepherd and I want to protect you; I want to love and care for your soul—but first you must come to me so that we can walk side by side," what do you do?

Do you come?

I was raised with no religious background. But in the silence of my own personal cell, I heard his voice and followed it.

~

My eyes flashed open in the cool, dark dungeon. The clock read 7:00 a.m. I had been in bed since 9:00 p.m., sleeping with my arms crossed in an attempt to channel warmth. But the thin mattress lay close to the ground, and no amount of holding myself comforted me in this meager bed.

My eyes rested on the falling snow through the window. My insides felt like frozen rain—cold, diminishing, falling, melting. I drifted back to sleep.

In my dream I was falling through the same black trajectory. Flashes of light struck me in the face, blinding me, bruising me. I groped for anything to hold on to, even the cameras that repelled me, but I lost my grip and my hands slipped from them.

A long strip of spiraling negatives curled toward me from the darkness, wrapping itself around my ankles, coiling around my body like a carnivorous snake. It tied my arms and made its way around my neck, tightening its grip with every coil. Barely able to breathe, I fell faster and faster, the speed numbing my body, the screams of countless women thundering in my ears.

Then I saw my little Bosquo. Her bones protruded from her body; her hair was sparse and short. She was clawing at the ground, unable to lift her head; a pool of blood surrounded her. She was so weak and emaciated that she couldn't move, and I couldn't get to her.

In the dream, the fury of the fall seemed like it would never end, but then I saw a tree sticking out of the tunnel. Inching my arms out of the ties that bound me, I hurled my body toward the tree and clutched onto a branch. Clamoring toward the trunk, I wrapped my arms around it—it was a lifeline. Gasping for air, I yanked the film from my neck and threw it into the void.

"Bosquo! Bosquo! Where are you?" I cried. But there was only emptiness, *niente*, nothing.

"Get up," a voice said, breaking through the rapture of my sleep.

"It's warm under the blankets, and it's cold out there," was my reply as I turned over and shut my eyes again.

"Jennifer, get up," the voice repeated, stronger and harder than before. It came from the window. I had never heard a voice like that before; it was so commanding, so sure.

As I threw back the blankets, I remembered a little verse I learned in my studies of Italian: *La luce è più forte dell'oscurità*, the light is stronger than the dark. Was it true?

"I have to get up," I said aloud.

I showered, dressed, put on my makeup, and went outside. I figured that I might as well go to my casting. I took the metro to a stop just outside the center of the city.

This was odd to me. All my life, I had been told not only that I *could* sell my beauty, but also that I *should*! No one had ever before told me *not* to.

As I walked down a long, wide, concrete boulevard, the steeples and clock towers of the city loomed ahead. I was trudging along when I realized how starkly barren the road was. It had no grass, no trees, no life, no animals, nothing. There were only a few papers strewn on the ground and some random businessmen walking stolidly along, holding their briefcases, their faces devoid of life.

Then suddenly a strange man standing on the side of the road appeared before me. He raised his hand like a policeman to stop me.

I stopped. "*No speakanse Deutsch*," I told him. I *don't* speak German!

The man was wearing a red jockey's coat, black knickers, socks pulled to his knees, and a cap—it looked like an Austrian war general's—pulled taught over his silver curly hair. He had big, dancing blue eyes, and behind him leaned an antiquated black bicycle that looked like it had been time-warped from my grandmother's era.

"*Parlez-vous français?*" He asked if I spoke French.

"No," I answered. "*Parlate italiano?*" Maybe he knew Italian.

"No," was his answer. Again he asked, "*Вы говорите русского?*"

"Do I speak Russian? I think not! *¿Hablas español?*" I asked, knowing Spanish was a long shot, but I had to try.

"No!" he grunted in frustration. Waving his hands about, finally he yelled at me, "My dear, what are you doing here?"

"Yes! Yes! I speak English!"

"You are English?" he asked, astounded.

"No, no, I am American!" I was excited now.

"Then why aren't you in America?"

"Uh…" I didn't exactly know how to answer that question.

"Are you studying here?"

"No."

"Are you traveling?"

"Not really…" I never liked telling people I was a model—I just wasn't proud of it.

"Are you here with your family?"

"No…" I wasn't sure why I was answering his questions, but I felt I was supposed to for some reason.

His brow converged, and he looked me up and down. I was wearing my standard modeling gear: boots, stockings, miniskirt, and sweater, while carrying my leather backpack that held my portfolio.

"Oh no," he groaned. "You are not *modeling* here, are you?"

"Yes, I am," I answered, feeling suddenly ashamed.

"My dear!" he exclaimed. Then he looked me square in the eye and stated emphatically, "You cannot *sell* your beauty!"

This was the oddest statement to me. All my life, I had been told that I *could* sell my beauty. Not only that I could, but also that I should! No one had ever told me this before. It completely threw me off.

"Where are you going now?" he asked with an air of wariness.

"To a casting," I said quietly.

"What is that?"

"I go to meet the clients," I explained. "I show them my pictures, and they decide if they want to hire me."

"My dear, you cannot sell your face!" he seemed almost outraged. "Do not go to them! They should come to you!"

"Excuse me?"

"Don't you see?" he said, looking as if he might shake me at any moment. "You go to them, they buy your face and body, and they use it like a piece of—of *furniture*! This is terrible."

My voice cracked as I said, "I know. I—I don't even want to do it anymore." I covered my face with my hands.

He put a warm hand on my shoulder. "Oh, my dear! What have they done to you? Have they hurt you?"

"No, no. No one has hurt me." I had become so accustomed to maintaining this image, this "perfect" path. It would be *years* until I was able to fully recall all that had happened and the many ways in which they had hurt me.

"If they have not hurt you," he asked, "then why do you cry?"

"I don't know," I said, "I think I just miss my family...I miss my grandmother."

"Then turn around now, before it is too late!" the man cried out, pointing his finger in the direction I had come. "Call the airlines, *now*! Book your plane ticket and go back to America, where you belong! Your family needs you! Your grandmother needs you!"

"But—but I have plans. I'm going to travel," I didn't know what else to say to him.

"Where? Where is better to go than your home?"

"I was thinking of going to Spain, Portugal, maybe even Prague. This is my chance to travel and see things." Isn't that what my parents and others had been telling me?

"No Spain, no Portugal, no Prague. My dear, don't travel. *Go home!*"

"I was going to see the Black Forest before I went home." I don't know what my fascination was with the Black Forest—maybe it was from reading *Hansel and Gretel* as a child.

"The Black Forest," he relented, to my surprise. "OK, it is beautiful. See it if you must. But if you really want to see something spectacular before you leave, you should go to *Zugspitze*," he said. "The highest mountain in all of Munchen! *That* is worth seeing.

"But then you must promise me that you will return to America, where you belong."

I nodded. It seemed bizarre to take such life-changing direction from a stranger. But somehow I knew I could trust what I saw in his eyes. They were kind and clear.

"Remember, my dear," he said again, putting his hand on my shoulder and gently turning me around, "you should *not* go to them; they should come to you. Someday people will come to hear what *you* have to say. *Many* will come! Trust me; you will see."

I thanked him, said good-bye, and walked back the way I had come.

And I never took another picture for money.

~~~

I did not go straight home after talking with the man I met on the street. I had one more appointment to keep. A photographer wanted me to do a job in Milan the week of the launch party for Damien's new magazine with me on the cover. So I prayed that whatever path God wanted me to take would be obvious. If I was not supposed to return to Milan, the photographer would not give me the job. If I was supposed to return, I would show my face then return home.

On my way to the casting, there was a skip in my step already, because I trusted the route would be laid out for me. I did not worry anymore about which road to take.

As it turned out, the photographer wanted me to do the job but refused to pay my train ticket to and from Milan. "There's my answer," I thought. I was not going to Milan. I certainly wasn't going to pay my way!

"God bless you," I said to the photographer, shaking his hand and looking him straight in the eye. He was taken aback. I guess, like myself, he had never heard anyone in the business utter those words.

On the way home I stopped at a kiosk and bought *two* Snickers bars—yes, *two!* I was done with modeling! I was free. And now, I was going to eat! And *enjoy* it! *Whoo-hoo!*

I ran as fast as I could along the icy sidewalk back to 66 *Rosenheimerstrasse.*

There was a package on the doorstep when I got back to the apartment. I already knew what it contained. I knew that within the thick brown paper, taped oh, so meticulously, was a little miracle just for me. It was the answer—the big answer—to the prayers I had said: "I don't really believe in you, God. If you can hear me, prove yourself. If you are real, then show yourself."

My heart pounded and *leapt* as I tore open the wrapping. There it was: my yellow journal, bright gold, and shimmering as the sun.

As fast as I could, I turned to the last page. There, in careful writing, I read a letter from the gentleman who found it. The letter was in Italian and I couldn't understand all of it, but I got the gist. He was fascinated by my story; he would love to meet me one day and also would love, of course, to meet Bosquo!

During one of those foggy winter days in Munich, I had received a phone call from my agency in Milan. They said a man had written them a letter, saying he had found a yellow journal under a seat on a train when he was traveling from Naples to Reggio di Calabria, the tip of the toe in the Italian "boot." Imagine, three hundred miles south from where it had been stolen, a man who both read and spoke English found my journal.

After reading the journal from cover to cover, he had only one way to trace me: a scrawled address on one page. In a handwritten letter to the mysterious address, he asked if they knew a girl with a little dog, who might have lost a yellow journal, and who signed her name with a *j.*

"Could that be you?" the guy from the agency in Milan had asked.

"That's me! That's my journal!" I cried as my eyes began stinging with tears. I must have written down the agency's address on one of the pages! I could hardly believe it!

"With these pages I will write my first book," I had told a friend of mine one day, many moons ago.

And what about the man who found it? Yes, I spoke with him on the phone and thanked him greatly. His name—*Sergio Leggere*—means "one who reads."

Inside the apartment, with my decision made, I stripped off my coat and scarf, pulled out my suitcase, and did what I had wanted to do for so long. It was a day I had dreamt of for years: the day I quit modeling. In the bottom of the suitcase I put my portfolios, fancy shoes, clothes, and makeup.

Then I packed a little backpack with my journal, some hiking boots, and my Good News Bible. On the way to the train station, I stopped only to toss my size 4 miniskirt into the Dumpster. I would never need that again! It was like a thousand tons were lifted from my shoulders.

Zugspitze, here I come!

⁓

As the sun sprayed honey-sweet light on the morning sky, I set out for the snowy mountain. At the edge of town, the road dissolved into several trails that branched off into the woods. I could choose any of them. Standing still, I looked down at my trusty brown hiking boots and considered my options.

Eyes scanning the wide trails, I saw how beautiful they were with the snow sparkling like diamonds on the surface of the well-established footpaths. A narrow path caught my eye; it was not as well traveled, but its rich, brown soil showed through the freshly fallen snow. It looked solid. I glanced up at the mountain. The top of *Zugspitze* looked like a piece of chocolate pie doused with a dollop of whipped cream.

On instinct, I took the narrow path, and with each stride, grew in certainty that I had chosen the right one. As the sun rose higher and higher in the sky, the snow glistened like crystals and towering pines cast shadows on the trail. Climbing over rocks and roots and around overgrown bushes that impeded the narrow, curvy path, I made sure to stay on the marked route. I walked all morning, making my way higher and higher up the mountain. The cold air refreshed and exhilarated me; it tasted like a drink of clean water, and breathing became a delight.

My smile grew, my lungs expanded, and my steps quickened as I traversed the switchbacks—back and forth, back and forth—long stretches, wide curves, long stretches, narrow curves. Believe it or not, in the forests of Germany you will find small wooden crosses nailed to the tree trunks, representing Jesus's body crucified.

With a sudden burst of energy, I began running, whipping past the crosses, and Jesus was everywhere I looked, at every turn, every bend—he was there. The crosses were whizzing by me in a blur and yet searing themselves into my heart, breath, and mind.

I came upon a clearing, a giant, rippling white blanket of snow that looked like someone had shaken it out and laid it down just for me. My legs sunk knee-deep in powder as I tried to run across. Fumbling along, I managed to make my way to a little hillock and sat down in the snow beneath a tree. I lay down and looked up at the sky.

Tired, I closed my eyes, thinking, "I can go to sleep here; maybe I'll freeze to death and never wake up. No one even knows exactly where I am." As I lay there, immobile, I felt my body grow numb from the cold. Then I realized I had another choice. I could open my eyes and live; I could start over.

My eyes pried open; some dark clouds shifted, then passed over the sun. A breeze stirred, touching my forehead. "Come in," I whispered. "Come in, Jesus."

God is not trying to exclude anyone! He wants no one to die separated from him. But if they won't listen when he calls, they won't *listen.*

It was as if that little girl inside me tiptoed through the house of my heart and quietly opened the door to him. As she opened it, the first gray cloud exited, the wind carried it away, and light streamed in. I inhaled a long, fresh, clean breath.

I began wedging my arms in and out, in and out, making angels in the snow just as I used to do in the sand as a girl. I would comb the white crystals with my hands while I listened to the deafening roar of the waves pounding the shore.

Wearing my blue and white polka-dot bathing suit, I would play on the beach for hours. Mom, her tan, freckled skin hot in the sun, lay on a chaise lounge and read magazines, looking up every few minutes. She would watch me chase the waves, laugh, let them catch me on their way back, and squeal from the cold water washing over my feet. And I spent endless time building sand castles decorated with seashells and would run to show her—my blonde hair bouncing in pigtails, my fair skin and blue eyes sparkling in the sun.

Without thought, I stood up and began to play in the snow. I used my bare hands to build a little snowman with rocks for eyes and a twig for a pipe. Then I ran, stumbling, laughing, across the soft, deep, pure white blanket. Turning, I headed down the mountain, swift as a horse on a rocky trail, letting my heart fly loose on the wind.

The words I had read in *Martin Eden* finally came true for me: "[My] feet were no longer clay, and [my] flesh became spirit; before [my] eyes and behind [my] eyes shone a great glory; and then the scene before [me] vanished and [I] was away, rocking over the world that to me was a very dear world."[1]

At the base of *Zugspitze*, in my little room at the bed-and-breakfast, there was a desk and a bed. Above the bed was a white horse galloping on the beach, water spraying from its hooves. I had found my horse. I had mounted. I was riding, fast and free.

IT'S IN THE WORD

The wide road beckons all our lives. It says: come, explore, taste, and see—the world is good.

Yes, the world *is* good. It is a fascinating plethora of tastes and sights and sounds that make your heart tear in agony and soar in ecstasy. God does not say the world is not good. On the contrary, he says his creation *is* good (Gen. 2:31). But he never says it will satisfy our longings.

What is it that you long for? The perfect path? The right route to take? The way you should go? That was one of the things I constantly wondered: *where to next?*

Those who choose the wide road—and I was certainly one of them—may have a breadth of experience, but they do not necessarily have the depth of solid truth to stand on. There is a reason why Jesus says the world is sinking sand and he is the rock. (See Matthew 7:24–27.) The world will suck you up. The world will promise that freedom is having sex when and with whom you choose, going wherever you want and whenever you want, experimenting with drugs and alcohol, and indulging your every whim and desire. The world will even tell you that beauty can be constructed by someone in a sterile surgical gown. It will promise you that money will buy satisfaction and religion is what *you* make it. But all of these things are lies; they end in destruction.

Those on the wide road have what I call a wide, shallow faith. It is made up of a conglomeration of "all roads lead to God," so whatever they *want* to believe is "truth." If you believe that 2 + 3 = 10, does that make it true? Of course not! But when it comes to religion, the world says truth is relative—it's whatever you believe it is. Truth is what feels good to you. So if you mix together a little Buddhism, a little idol worship, a little bit of Jesus—and maybe a little of whatever else you theorize as truth when you are high or meditating—then that is truth, for today.

Then maybe tomorrow 2 + 3 + 1 will equal 10 because you have found a new philosophy to add to your truth. You have found a new teacher with a new teaching. See, it is a wide path; it draws from a lot of different sources.

As the Father who loves you, God wants you to know that the wide road is destructive. It is that simple. He asks you to come to the narrow road because it leads to life.

If you ask someone on the wide road—as I once was asked—"What is truth? What do you believe?" there will be a fumbling, theorizing, long-winded, circular answer. Why? Because their path is not a clear one; it is confusing, even to them.

Jesus is the narrow road. He *is* narrow. He said it himself when he told us, "I am the way and the truth and the life. No one comes to the Father except through me" (John 14:6). He also said, "I am the gate; whoever enters through me will be saved" (John 10:9). That's narrow! You don't get a narrower path than that.

But Jesus is also endlessly deep. His path is one that goes back since the beginning of time. God promised a Savior to Eve after the Fall. But even *before* that, Jesus Christ was with God; he was God. Then, when the time was right, he was with us; God became human. The Word (Jesus) became flesh, and he walked among us. (See John 1:1–10.)

The main complaint about Christianity—aside from the criticism that Christians are just as fallible and imperfect as non-Christians...so shocking...so true!—is that it is too narrow. It is "exclusive." The world cries, "A good God would not exclude people based on the fact that they don't accept his Son!"

But here's the truth: God sent his Son as an *invitation* to a relationship with him. No matter how other people behave, that does not change the fact that God wants us to have a relationship with him! He created us. He loves us. He wants us to know him—so badly that the Creator of the universe lowered himself to become a created being. And in the form of his Son, he walked among us, ultimately displaying the depth of his love in an emotionally and physically brutal death. What more could we want?

God is not trying to exclude anyone! He wants no one to die separated from him (2 Pet. 3:9). He doesn't want his children, his wandering sheep, to be devoured by wolves. But if they won't listen to him when he calls, they *won't* listen.

As the Father who loves you, God wants you to know that the wide road is destructive. It is that simple. He asks you to come to the narrow road because it leads to life—"life to the full." But he will not force you to come. He will not force you to accept and live the abundant, meaningful life he has in store for those who believe in him. That is your free will, your choice.

Personally, I am not going to argue with the Creator of the universe about a better way. I have walked too many dead-end paths to tell him that my way is better. And he *has* proven himself to me.

In the past twelve years of following Christ, he has yet to lead me down a path of darkness. Any paths of darkness I have walked down have been from my own stubborn pride, wondering if possibly the wide road was better at the time. Each time, I had to humbly crawl back to the narrow road and drink from the waters of his love. Then he stood me back up to walk by his side.

Of course, he always makes me better for having fallen. That's the beauty of the narrow path: he's there to pick you up and dust you off when you fall.

Psalm 1, which Shane and I read at our wedding, says those who choose not to walk the wide road will be blessed. After so many years of walking that wide road, we believed this with a very deep conviction. According to the psalm, the man or woman who walks the *narrow* road, however, delighting in the Word of God, will be "like a tree planted by streams of water, which yields its fruit in season and whose leaf does not wither. Whatever he does prospers" (Ps. 1:1–3).

A tree with shallow roots will not bear fruit. But a tree that plants itself by a deep stream of living water will have roots that are constantly nourished. That tree will bear fruit. According to John 15, that tree will be pruned—in other words, we will have trials—but it, in turn, will be stronger and ultimately produce more fruit.

In John 15, Jesus says he is the vine and we are the branches. If we hang on to the vine, he promises we will bear much fruit. Without him, "we can do nothing" (John 15:5). Without the water, the tree bears no fruit; without the vine, the branch bears nothing. What is the fruit? It is the peace we are looking for, the love we long for, the joy we so want! The desires of our hearts: that's the fruit! It all comes from him, the One who created it all.

In the words of Robert Frost:

> Two roads diverged in a wood, and I—
> I took the one less traveled by,
> And that has made all the difference.[2]

Taking the path of Christ has made all the difference for me. He is the perfect path because he is the path alongside the water. When we root ourselves in him, his path leads to a fruitful life. Not a perfect life; that is promised to no man. But, instead, it is a *fruitful* life. Think Thanksgiving; think a cornucopia, a basket overflowing with vibrant fruits and vegetables and grains of every texture and color. Think *abundance*.

This is what I have in my life today. It did not happen overnight, but it happened. Jesus has given me life to the full: one with an abundance of joy, peace for the asking, and love—those three things that I longed for, even as a little girl.

Of course, there have been seasons of grief, heartbreak, loss, disappointment, even misery; there has been suffering. But at the root of it all I have always had access to the source of joy, peace, and love—I have stayed attached to the vine (Jesus), connected to the water, and fruit has bloomed in season. In fact, it seems to get richer every year.

Are you looking for the perfect path? Look no longer. It begins on your knees or on your back or on your feet—by a river, by a lake, on a mountain, on an island, in your backyard, in a bookstore, or in your home. Above all, it begins in your heart, when that little girl—or little boy—inside of you opens the door so the Light can stream in.

Here I am! *I stand at the door and knock. If anyone hears my voice and opens the door, I will come in* and eat with him, and he with me.

—REVELATION 3:20, EMPHASIS ADDED

Enter through the narrow gate. For wide is the gate and broad is the road that leads to destruction, and many enter through it. *But small is the gate and narrow the road that leads to life.*

—MATTHEW 7:13–14, EMPHASIS ADDED

He calls his own sheep by name and leads them out… his sheep follow him because *they know his voice.*

—JOHN 10:3–4, EMPHASIS ADDED

I will lead them beside streams of water on a level path where they will not stumble.…They will be like a well-watered garden, and they will sorrow no more.

—JEREMIAH 31:9, 12, EMPHASIS ADDED

The man who looks intently into the perfect law that gives freedom, and continues to do this, not forgetting what he has heard, but doing it—*he will be blessed in what he does.*

—JAMES 1:25, EMPHASIS ADDED

Chapter 9

THE PERFECT FULFILLMENT

The Road to Healing

*A*s I check into a hostel set deep in the Black Forest, I'm grateful that Michael, the German man who gave me the Bible in the park, is storing my suitcase. He plans to pick me up at the train station when I return to Munich. At least now someone knows where I am. When I told him that I accepted Christ at Zugspitze, he had me go to church and pray with the pastor before leaving, a strange formality to me at the time. But now I know that he wanted me to understand the true meaning of Christ's blood in my life: that I was finally forgiven and forever free.

On day one, I walk along the Danube River, the cold wind driving against my face. The Black Forest in February is dark, wet, foggy, packed with snow, and astonishingly beautiful. On the horizon of the mountain vista I see a cross, at first hidden by haze and then clear as could be. I am fasting while I am here—this is so drastic a turn for me. I need time to process and, most importantly, finish reading this book tucked in my back pocket, the pages that are resuscitating my soul.

On day two, I rent a bike and ride the trails along the icy blue Danube, wild and rushing. Something is still wrong with me though. My body throbs, my skin is still ravaged with bulbous sores, and my stomach is restless, painful, churning. I am drinking tea that the kind woman from the agency gave me—she said it would cleanse my system and clear my skin.

On day three, I take a train to the next town and find it desolate. While sitting on a bridge, feet dangling over the water, I hear bells tolling in the distance. Then a boy races by me in long strides, with a book in his hand. Curious, I follow him to a church square where the townspeople have gathered. I file in with them and sit down, not comprehending a word of the sermon except "Jesus," yet I weep the entire time, tears streaming down my face as I bow my head so that no one can see me.

A Word About Fasting

Fasting is a biblical practice in which one denies oneself of food for a period of time to concentrate on spiritual matters. The last thing I really should have been doing at this time was fasting, because I was already dangerously thin and suffering from an eating disorder. Nevertheless, fasting can be a way to help you focus on God when done for the right reason—which is to draw near to him. As you will read, God blessed my fast and used this time to heal me of the "wildly disordered" mind I was experiencing.

Jesus is not without compassion. He took time to speak to a widow at Nain. The Bible says, "When the Lord saw her, his heart went out to her and he said, 'Don't cry'" (Luke 7:13).

When he "saw her."

Another verse says, in the midst of her despair, Hagar called him, "The God who sees me" (Gen. 16:13). I had realized on Zugspitze that he was the only One who could see me. Now I wonder: if he sees me, can he fix me too?

"Heal me," I whisper. "Please, heal me."

When I look in the mirror at the hostel, the windows of my soul—my eyes—are still markedly dark. There is barely a glimmer buried beneath the many layers. Something in my stomach wrestles. "What's wrong with me, God?" I question.

Night after night, I read by the light of a candle. The hostel is empty, as I am the only one crazy enough to come here in the thick of winter. I sip cup after cup of tea. But really I am living off the brown, tattered pages of this little Good News Bible, my soul absorbing each word like bits of Communion bread.

I am drawn by stories of men and women who were rejected by people and embraced by God. When people disappoint, scorn, judge, reject, condemn, and belittle, Jesus touches, has compassion for, heals, forgives, drives out demons, and frees.

I think about Kim, the girl in Siena, who told me, "If you want to be healed, you must pray in the name of Jesus."

On day four, I walk too far in the woods and, in a rush to head back, end up at a dead end on the wrong side of the river. The sun is sinking in the sky, and I'll be caught miles from the hostel if I don't go forward. I do not have the time to run back to the place where I can cross the water. So I slide down a steep bank, and pace up and down the shore looking for the narrowest spot. I dip my boot into the icy Danube, checking for depth. The water is biting cold, but I think I can make it across. I know it's crazy, but I don't have a choice. I can't stop the sun from setting, and I'm running out of time.

Midway, I am up to my hips feeling like I'm going to freeze, and the current is stronger than it was by the shore.

If I lose my footing, I could easily be swept away; I could die here.

It crosses my mind to wonder what my parents would think now. I am in a river, in a large forest, in the middle of an unfamiliar country, on a different continent, on the other side of the world; they can't see me or hear my cries.

"God, don't let me go now," I pray. "Help me!"

"When you pass through the waters, I will be with you; and when you pass through the rivers, they will not sweep over you." Years later I would read Isaiah 43:2 and my chin would drop in awe.

I reach the bank on the other side, and, although it is only knee-deep, it's rocky; the current sweeps me off my feet and I fall back into the river. It takes me only a few yards and I dive for a rock, clamoring breathlessly onto the bank, body prostrate. I take off my wet glove and, in shaking it, lose it in a piles of leaves. I have to find it; my hand will freeze!

I check my back pocket. My Bible is gone too—my food!

I can get stuck in the forest at night; I can find a way back. But I cannot, I will not, go on without the Word.

After a few minutes of searching, I hear a crow caw on the other side of the river. It must have fallen out when I slid down the bank. I can't cross that river again; my feet will freeze.

The sky cracks and it begins to rain. With numb feet sloshing around in drenched hiking boots, wet jeans, one glove, and a desperate spirit, I sprint back along the shore of the river, keeping one eye on the setting sun. The rain and the wind drive hard at me, but after about a mile I get back to the place I can cross. I do, then I run another mile or so back to the bank, sliding down it once again. In a mad search against the growing darkness I scan the purple, brown, and gold leaves, and then step on it. I step on that tender book, lying quietly at the side of the rushing water, waiting for me.

I tuck it into my chest, clamor up the bank, and walk briskly back to a little town that sits on that side of the woods. It's dark now and the rain is coming in buckets, but I am deliriously happy. I beg for coins, duck into a phone booth, and call the man from the hostel. When his car pulls up, I realize he must think I'm crazy. I am crazy; I have gone crazy mad. I am quaking and wet to the bone. But I am a survivor. And I have my food.

What We're Really Longing For

Fulfillment: *the state of being fulfilled, satisfied, or complete; developed to full potential*

We are born with longings. We long for love, peace, happiness, hope, and a future. We long to be known, seen, loved, and, above all, we long to be healed and fulfilled. These longings become caverns within us if they are not satisfied.

Beth Moore, who has taught me more about authentic faith than anyone, says the empty places within us are carved by three primary hands: a hand withheld, a hand lost, and the hand of God. By a hand withheld, she means that when we do not have the security and protection we so need, it carves within us an empty place that longs to be filled. By a hand lost, she means that when we lose someone or something precious to us, it also creates a cavern within. And by the hand of God, she means that he carved the empty place inside us with his own hand, purposefully creating a space only he can fill.[1]

These empty places—no matter how much we try to fill them with people or things—can only be filled by the living water of God. Without the pouring in of his Spirit, *nothing* can fill them; the empty places will forever contain gaps that remain vacant.

At one point in my journey in the Black Forest, I came upon a rusted, dried-up well. Next to it, there was a pond where people had tossed in their pennies as wishes.

In John chapter 4, Jesus went to the well because he was tired and thirsty from a long journey—the same reason why so many of us finally break down and go to the well. It's amazing how many *refuse* to go the wellspring of life, until they are so dry and cracked inside they can't even imagine what water would taste like, while other people quietly dip their ladle in the waters of God all their lives and remain refreshed.

In the biblical account, a woman walks up to the well to get some water. She doesn't go in the morning or in the evening when it is customary, but in the middle of the day—probably to avoid running into people who know her reputation.

Sitting down by the well, Jesus asks her for a cup of water.

Every time I drink deep from his Word and fill those empty places, they eventually get so filled up that they overflow.

Stunned that he would even speak to her—Jews and Samaritans hated each other and didn't intermix—she questions him, "How can you ask me for a drink?" (John 4:9). I'm sure she wonders why he wants to talk to a *woman*.

Jesus answers, "If you knew…who it is that asks you for a drink, you would have asked him and he would have given you *living water*" (v. 10, emphasis added).

Then she tries to argue with him that he doesn't even have a cup!

But Jesus isn't moved. He says, "Everyone who drinks this water will be thirsty again, but whoever drinks the water I give him will never thirst. Indeed, the water I give him will become in him a spring of water welling up to eternal life" (vv. 13–14).

Then it all comes out in the open—she has been with many men, and the man she is with now isn't her husband. She has tried everything possible to fill her empty places (vv. 16–19).

Why does Jesus tell *her* this story? Why doesn't he tell about the living water to the demon-possessed man, to the blind, poor, sick, or lame? Why *her*?

Because he knows her thirst. He knows her hunger. And he knows that he is the only source who can fill it. He is the source from which she was made, and he is the source from which she needs to drink to feel *full*. Jesus is saying to her, "Sweetheart, stop trying to fill your empty places with men." To us, he is saying, "Stop trying to fill your empty places with food, sex, alcohol, plans to travel, spending, running, money, drugs, dieting, or relationships. What you need is me. You need a well that doesn't run dry, a love that doesn't run out, and water that will truly satisfy."

Salvation, Beth Moore points out, is very different than satisfaction.[2]

The woman leaves her water jar at the well, goes back to the town, and says to the people, "Come, see a man who told me everything I ever did. Could this be the Christ?" (v. 29).

Why does she leave her water jar? Because she realizes that she has found the source that will fill her "empty place"—a man who knows everything she ever did and does not judge her. He does not ask anything of her. He only offers *free fulfillment*.

Later in John, Jesus says he has food to eat that his disciples know nothing about. He calls himself "the Bread of Life" and "the Living Water" (John 4:10–13; 6:33, 35, 48, 51).

In the Black Forest of Germany, he became my bread and water. He still is.

Practically speaking, today we have access to God's living water through the Bible. It is our bread, our food. It is the perfect law that gives freedom, the only perfect on Earth. It is the place we go to refill our hearts—and it is best to go daily instead of waiting until we're running on empty. When the imperfections of life on Earth begin to eat me alive, I realize I haven't spent enough time allowing him to fill the empty places.

Over our stove at home, an artist painted a cornucopia of abundance and our family motto: "Our cup runneth over." The painting was a housewarming gift to Shane and me from our parents. The saying comes from Psalm 23:

> The Lord is my shepherd, I shall not be in want. He makes me lie down in green pastures; he leads me beside quiet waters, he restores my soul. He guides me in paths of righteousness, for his name's sake. Even though I walk through the valley of the shadow of death, I will fear no evil, for you are with me; your rod and your staff, they comfort me. You prepare a table before me…you anoint my head with oil, *my cup overflows.*
> —Psalm 23:1–5, emphasis added

What begins to happen—and it happens more and more for me now—is that every time I drink deep from his Word and fill those empty places, they eventually get so filled up that they overflow. I am not trying to suck everything and everyone around me dry while trying to fill me, because I'm already full. I don't worry so much about *myself* anymore; I have become much more interested in pouring his love out to others.

From My World to Yours

The truth is, God satisfies the desires of every living thing. If you delight yourself in him, he will give you the desires of your heart, as he did for me (Ps. 145:16, 37:4). He will fill your longings—no matter how they were carved.

No one wants to be just a face on a wall, a face on a card. You have a heart and soul; you want to be known, seen, and loved. "With the skill of a craftsman," God says, "I wove you together in the depths of the earth; I formed your innermost parts." (See Psalm 139:13–15.) He does know you. In fact, he knows you better than anyone because he made you. And when he made you, he carved a certain place in your heart that only he can fill.

He knows your longings because he created them. And he offers you the only thing that will fill that God-shaped hole in your little-girl heart: the truth that you are loved with a perfect, undying love; that you are beautiful and worth fighting for; that he will never leave you or betray you; and that there is a future in store for you beyond your wildest dreams. In his Son, God promises all these things.

When you are in the thick of the forest, the middle of the current that you so fear might sweep you away, he sees you; his heart goes out to you, and he wants nothing more than to reach out his hand and help you, if you would only reach back.

Finally, he wants to fill your deepest, deepest longing: to be healed.

On the fifth day of my trip to the Black Forest, I sat in a tiny slat of sunlight on a shaded bank, tired but unable to rest. I remembered Kim telling me I had to pray in the name of Jesus and how I hadn't believed her. Well, I believed her now.

Like a desperate, hungry, needy beggar of a child, I crawled along the rocky soil onto the pathway.

From the very core of me came a deep wail, a long, choking sob. It emptied me out, and I landed on the ground.

My cheek was pressed hard to the rocky path. I cried, the tears coming from the center of that little girl inside me who had gone into the world in search of perfect. Her heart lay in shards all over the ground.

There was a growing warmth on the back of my neck. Slowly, I dared to look up. The dark clouds had opened, and the sun beamed through as if riding on a chariot. In the snowy, frozen winter of the lightless forest, *the sun was shining on me.*

Then I sensed a voice, not booming, not thundering, just still and sure: "My daughter, you are healed. You may go in peace." The voice came from my heart, and I knew it was true.

I wiped the grit of broken rocks off my slobbery cheek, staggering up like a colt trying to rise. Stumbling forward in the forest, I saw a hillside off to the right, basked in light. I climbed up and sat. The sun shone on me, warming my shoulders, face, and body. I couldn't remember the last time the sun warmed me like this. It reminded me of my backyard at home, the way I felt bathed in light.

I faded off in memory, able again to remember myself as a child.

When I was a little girl I had sapphire eyes and porcelain skin. Wide-eyed and wild about the world around me, I loved nothing more but to run barefoot on the warm, tickly grass of our backyard. Greg and I played imaginary games in the massive arms of the oak trees, fished for crawdads in the trickling creek bed behind the yard, and swung from a rope vine that hung from the arching limb of a giant oak. I always loved the thrill of slipping my foot into the loop of the rope, jumping off the bank, and sailing over the marsh below, twirling, laughing, head thrown back, free. I can still feel the cool, moist air on my flushed cheek; hair flipping in the breeze; eyes watering from the sheer exhilaration of it all. The sweet nectar of childhood.

At last, sitting on that sunlit bank of the Black Forest, I was quiet now. After days of unrest, I was finally still. And the strangest thing was, I felt full. I felt young again. I felt free.

When I got up, my first instinct was to run. My next instinct was to go home—by train, by plane, by car, it didn't matter—I had to get back to my backyard.

And that's exactly what I did, in that order.

~~~

In the early morning, I walked to the front desk of the hostel to check out. I had just enough money to pay for five nights—I had dared not bring any more cash along for my trip to the Black Forest for fear that weakness would drive me to quit the fast. I held my prepaid train ticket in hand. But, strangely enough, the foyer of the hostel was packed with people that morning.

There had been *no one* in the hostel for five days, and now there was a crowd?! I stood in line for ten minutes, fearing I'd miss my train—the *only* train going to Munich that day—if I waited any longer. Finally, I pushed ahead of the people, dropped my money on the proprietor's desk, and ran.

The power of the ice-cold wind and driving snow threatened to stop me as I ran as fast as I could toward the station. Panicking that I would miss my train, I tried to propel my legs forward, but I was too weak.

Forcing each stride, I pushed harder and harder against the powerful wind.

When I arrived, panting and out of breath, I raced to the window and showed the lady my train ticket. She shook her head and waved her hands in front of her face, saying, "*Der Zus ist weg! Der Zus ist weg!*"

I feared she was saying the train was gone, but I didn't want to believe it.

I raced to the platform anyway, but there was no train. My heart sank. I trudged back to the window and begged the woman to refund my ticket, but she refused, either because she didn't understand me or my prepaid ticket back to Munich was nonrefundable.

I was stranded in a little town called *Donaueschingen*, which I fondly like to call "Don't-know-nothing, Jen." I had no money left; I hadn't eaten in five days. A blizzard was kicking up outside, and I was hours away from anyone I knew.

I decided I had no choice but to hitchhike.

Standing in the whirling snow, I stuck out my thumb. Right away, a blue car pulled over, and the man inside spoke a little English. He said he couldn't take me to Munich, but he could take me to a place where I would likely find a ride.

> ### A Word About Hitchhiking
>
> Hitchhiking is very dangerous, and I was a fool to do this. Don't ever try it. I was lucky I didn't wind up dead.

I was stunned when he dropped me off on the shoulder of the *autobahn*—a super-wide highway in Germany that has no speed limit! Probably because people only took the *autobahn* for very long trips, and most people were on their way to work, it was practically deserted at this time of day. Every once in a while a car sped by me at some unbelievable speed, whipping up dirt and snow and water that sprayed in my face.

I jumped up and down to keep warm, pacing back and forth, wishing I had my missing glove because the fingers on my right hand were numb. Every time a big truck sped past, I turned around and pretended I was getting something out of my backpack, fearing that someone horrible would pick me up.

Finally, I got down on my knees on the icy, concrete shoulder of the highway and prayed, knowing this time I was being heard: "God, all I ask of you right now is a warm car and a kind person."

I stood up, and a few minutes later, a little white truck pulled over. I ran after it, and the door swung open. A surge of warmth poured from the car.

"Munchen?" the little old man behind the wheel asked.

"Yes! Yes! Munchen!" I said. "I'm going to Munich!"

He waved me inside. "*Ich bin Josef*," he said, telling me his name was Josef.

Josef had a crevassed face, silver hair, and sky blue eyes. He offered me a thermos of coffee. I smiled and declined, knowing that it would tear my stomach apart. But he was a kind person, and he kept offering it to me, again and again.

 When we are in the thick of the forest, in the middle of the current that we so fear might sweep us away, God sees us.

The drive took several hours. He spoke little English and I knew very little German, yet through a mesh of languages I still do not comprehend to this day, we chatted back and forth the whole trip. I learned about his family, and he, mine. As we talked, he kept opening up his lunchbox, offering me an extra sandwich, an apple, and a mint, over and over. I kept saying no, because I intended to fast for the rest of the day.

Then I looked out the window and saw that sun once again shining through those clouds, and I felt within me a truth, a finality, a sense of completion. It was this: *You are well. You are healed. Eat. It is over.*

It was over.

I turned back to look at Josef: he put a mint in his mouth and chewed it, rubbing his belly and nodding his head like a mother does to a child who doesn't want to eat. "*Es ist gut* [it is good]," he said, grinning from ear to ear.

I accepted it from him, which made him gleefully happy, and it burst with flavor in my mouth. After a while, he offered me his apple again, and then his sandwich. I accepted them both and ate slowly, thinking that this time it *was* good.

When we arrived in Munich, we hugged and said good-bye. But before I closed the car door, he took out another half sandwich, another apple, and the rest of his mints and handed them to me. I tried to refuse, but he wouldn't let me. It was like he *knew* that I needed to eat.

Then he opened his wallet, handing me *all* the money that was inside it. Of course I said, "No, Josef, no!" But he insisted I take it. How did he know I had no money? Not even for a phone call. He just *knew*.

Does God see you? Yes. Does God know you? Yes. Does God love you? Yes, he does. And does he hear you? Oh, yes, he hears you!

~~~

When I finally boarded a plane to the United States, I had no intention of ever speaking of all that happened. It seemed impossible. I couldn't explain to my family, even if I wanted to. I couldn't explain to my friends—who had spent their summers away from college relaxing in the safety of their homes, scooping up ice cream, waiting tables, or teaching dance. No, to try to even begin to explain, well, that just seemed like *too much*.

I wrote about it, in the quiet of my own heart, and in the stillness of the night and early morning. I wrote it all down in every minute detail. But I did not speak of it.

What I did speak of, though, was Christ. Most people thought I was totally insane to have walked away from such a glamorous, lucrative business, from a career that took me years to build, from a life that had taken me to places most people long to see. The majority of people I knew at home didn't read the Bible, didn't go to church, didn't "buy" all that. But I didn't care; if they asked, I told them, "It is God who saved me."

IT'S IN THE WORD

When Jesus healed Mary Magdalene of her demons, he broke every chain that bound her. She had to have been a mess—in her day, demon possession referred to some kind of mental imbalance, emotional infirmity, or physical disease that was difficult to explain. Most likely, the anxieties of life had taken her over, causing her to become estranged from her community and considered incurable—either on a physical, mental, emotional, or spiritual level, we don't know, but probably a combination of them all.

After Jesus healed her, she up and left everything—which I'm sure she considered nothing—to follow Christ. He healed her, and she followed him. It was as simple as that.

All the way from Galilee, she traveled with Jesus, providing for his needs as she watched him preach, teach, heal the sick, feed the hungry, and perform miracles (Luke 8:1–3). She had found the One who saw her need, heard her cries, healed her, and fulfilled her.

Then, before her very eyes, she saw the lover of her soul beaten, flogged, spat upon, ridiculed, and tortured. Even at the cross, when almost everyone else had fled, Mary stayed with him to hear his final words and witness his last breath (Luke 23:49; John 19:25).

Mary rose early the next morning and went to the tomb while it was still dark. But she found the tomb empty. She was weeping in bitter agony when the risen Lord appeared to her. "Mary," he said, calling her by name, just as he calls you by name, just as he called me by name.

"*Rabboni!*" she cried, trying to grab hold of him.

But he told her she could not hold on to him. Instead, she had to "go and tell." (See John 20:1–18.)

What else could she do? She had found the only One who would accept her as she was—riddled with demons and rejected by all—and he loved her like that. His love had filled her empty places.

It would only seem natural now that from the overflow of her heart, she would speak.

The law of the LORD is *perfect*, reviving the soul.
—PSALM 19:7, EMPHASIS ADDED

In the time of my favor *I will answer you*, and in the day of salvation *I will help you*; I will…say to the captives, "*Come out*," and to those in darkness, "*Be free!*" They will feed beside the roads and find pasture on every barren hill. They will neither hunger nor thirst…*He who has compassion on them will guide them and lead them beside springs of water.*
—ISAIAH 49:8–10, EMPHASIS ADDED

I have *heard* your prayer and *seen* your tears; *I will heal you.*
—2 KINGS 20:5, EMPHASIS ADDED

Jesus stood and said in a loud voice, "If anyone is thirsty, let him come to me and drink. Whoever believes in me, as the Scripture has said, *streams of living water will flow from within him.*"
—JOHN 7:37–38, EMPHASIS ADDED

Chapter 10

THE PERFECT FREEDOM

A Beautiful Mosaic

In mad passion I take an axe and whack at the poison ivy that's overtaken the creek bed. Bosquo, sweet, innocent, and on the mend from that run-in with the coyotes, stands back; she can see that I'm serious. With all my strength, I wallop the thorns and thistles, the briars and vines until I'm filthy and panting.

How could the running creek where I played as a child be so overgrown with that nasty red ivy? How could debris have clogged the creek in parts where it used to flow wild and free?

I'm living back at home now. Every day, while Mom and Dad are at work, Bosquo and I traverse the expanse of the lawn to climb across the creek so I can hack away. With shovel, rake, and hoe, I clear a big, wide section of soil, working it until it is rich and brown, fodder for something to grow.

I clean out the creek and tame the blackberry vines; I plant strawberries, tomatoes, lettuce, herbs, and flowers of all kinds, mostly from seed. As I watch my garden grow, I am careful to water, pull weeds, prune, and look for fruit. Most of all, I anticipate the joy of feeding my family with the harvest.

The flower shop where I work is in a small sidewalk hut along the coast of California. Each morning as I pull the cord and the blinds stack to the top of the pane, the light streams in and I look forward to the day ahead.

I remember the nights when I made my way back to that apartment in Milan—usually limping along from the blisters on my feet—I saw that vibrant girl at the flower shop. She wore no makeup and dressed in comfortable clothes. Her customers seemed to know her. Under the canopy of the little tin roof of that stand, she looked happy, safe. I wanted what she had: a simple life.

"Maybe I could work in a flower shop," I had told my brother one night when I called from Miami.

"A flower shop?" he questioned. "You didn't go to college to work in a flower shop, Jen."

"No, and I didn't go to college to pose for the camera either."

Now, each morning, I inhale the dense, sweet scent of flowers wafting through the air. Carefully, I place the best arrangements on the sidewalk and hang the trailing roses. The shop is quaint and has a very slow but steady stream of customers. I earn minimum wage selling someone else's flowers, but I don't worry about how I look, and I enjoy making arrangements that warm people's hearts.

In the complicated world of fashion and photography, I discovered that all I ever wanted was a simple life.

On my days off, I often go see Grandma, do her grocery shopping or cooking, rub her back, and take her to the doctor or to church. But most often, I just sit with her and sip a cup of tea, listening to stories about her life as a little girl growing up without a mother in the early 1900s.

Daily, I go for long walks with Bosquo. Eventually, I get a job working at a camp for kids, and Bosquo and I spend a summer in the mountains, soaking up every child's questions, discoveries, smiles, and hugs.

Then I take the money I made modeling and go back to school to become a writer.

What We're Really Longing For

Freedom: *the quality or state of being free; the absence of necessity, coercion, or constraint in choice or action; liberation from slavery, restraint, or from the power of another*

Faith gives us the freedom to be the girls God made—freedom to be a mess; freedom to be angry; freedom to be happy; freedom to be real; freedom to follow our hearts. Faith gave me freedom to leave it all—without a word of explanation to the many agencies around the world who expected me to be here, be there, do this, do that, look this way, look that way.

Faith gave me freedom to leave what so many believed was the perfect path. It freed me from caring what all those men in the modeling industry thought or even what people at home thought. It freed me to go without makeup, to eat again, and to fly, despite the low places I had been. It gave me dignity, worth, value. It made me stand tall. It freed me to go home, *imperfect*. It freed me from my sin, and it freed me to be me.

Freedom from "perfect," however, has come with time. God has broken the chains that bound my heart, painfully and slowly. Over time, he has also freed me to speak the truth of my life without fearing what people think.

I sat in my emerald green backyard, wearing an old patchwork dress, my unwashed hair tied back in a bun, my feet bare. I faced the sun. My limbs were outstretched, my stomach relaxed. I was still not completely well physically, but I was on the mend. My heart was at peace. I was ready for whatever life might bring, and finally I was not afraid.

Watching the shadows of the oak trees shift over the creek bed, I felt a sudden urge. I jumped up from the lawn and ran inside the house, grabbing a card table and chair, then dragging them out and setting them up in the yard. I ran back in and grabbed my laptop, an extension cord, and that cherished bright yellow journal.

As I flipped it open to page one and rested my fingers on the keyboard, I paused to close my eyes, to feel the sun heating my shoulders, to curl my toes into the soil beneath the warm, tickly grass. I said a silent prayer and began to write. I knew nothing about longings or Scripture. I only knew what happened, and I knew I must write it all down.

I kept pretending it was a story about some other girl with wild characters and crazy experiences. I pretended all the way through the first draft and the second. But it was *not fiction*; it was *all true*—and that realization at first was much too difficult for my young heart to manage.

When I saw that little girl as someone separate from myself—and at the same time, me—I felt such compassion and love toward her that I could not help but forgive her.

So I stuffed the pages in a drawer.

While studying writing in school, I turned my attention to mining ancient texts, studying the histories of biblical women, from Eve to Mary Magdalene…only to recognize my own life revealed in the biblical accounts of these women's lives. It was as if I saw my story in the pages of theirs. This discovery led me back to those pages in the drawer. Over the years I revisited them again and again, knowing that it was a story that couldn't be kept silent, for within it was the story of all women, their longings, their search for God, and their search to be healed, fulfilled, and free.

Deep down, those pages terrified me. I was so afraid that if I told the truth, if I shattered the images in my parents' and friends' and teachers' minds, then there wouldn't be anything left of me. They would see how imperfect I was beneath the masks.

"You *can* do this!" Shane told me a few years after we were married. "Don't let your fears stop you! I fell in love with this woman who was going to write this book! And you were going to give back to people with the story God gave you. So don't let your fear of failure stop you!"

I was standing with my back against my desk—my back against the wall. Our children, only one and three, were sleeping in the next room. "I can't do it," I cried. "I can't!"

"You can do it! You can!" he assured.

When I finally pulled out those pages and said yes, then, and only then, I found that little girl inside me again, the one created with intention and purpose, the one for whom God had a beautiful mosaic in mind.

Deep wounds, however, take time to heal. Medically speaking, some wounds cannot just be medicated and sewn closed. Sometimes raw wounds need to remain wide open for a long time, cleaned, and treated over and over until finally they are safe to be closed. They must heal from the inside out.

The "not speaking" of the pain in my heart proved to cause those wounds to fester more. I was quickly driven to tears, highly sensitive, and often afraid that I would be left alone. I had come to know the world as a frightening place, realizing that I could be its prey, and that made me insecure.

Throughout my twenties, I never felt beautiful enough; I always felt less than—less than perfect, less than worthy. Even when I began speaking publicly of my conversion, these secret fears stayed buried in my heart.

Through years of keeping too much masked, my health began to kick and rear. Long after my initial healing, the problems with my skin grew much, much worse. I also had constant pain in my neck and jaw.

After seeing many doctors, but only growing worse, I found a wise doctor who told me that I had to heal from something deeply buried in my heart, specifically, *the need to be perfect*. And if I would just *speak* of it—not publicly, but privately—the emotional healing would come and the physical would follow.

As I began to open my heart, mostly to God, but also to people, free, unconditional love was able to reach those empty places that I had long ago sewn closed. As I went to the deepest, furthest lesions within, finally giving them a voice, that love gently licked my wounds like a calm current of water lapping the shore. Over time, it smoothed out the most jagged pieces that once broke off my heart.

 Letting go of perfect is letting go of the temporary. It is getting our eyes off the demands of the world and fixing them on God, the only Perfect that lasts.

In the office of a wise counselor, I found forgiveness—oh, I had forgiveness from God many years earlier, in that forest. But I had not forgiven myself, so there were still tears in remembering certain times from Greece, Paris, Milan, and Munich. The counselor helped me see myself as that little girl in the world, looking for affirmation and acceptance, trying to maintain an image that wasn't real; that girl in search of the perfect dream, the perfect path, trying with all her might to find anything that would fill the longing.

When I saw that little girl as someone separate from myself—and at the same time, me—I felt such compassion and love toward her that I could not help but forgive her. I finally began to see myself as God sees me.

Snap, snap, snap went the chains that bound me...*snap, snap, snap*...and healing came in parts and pieces; freedom came in waves.

FROM MY WORLD TO YOURS

Can you see yourself as God sees you? Can you see the girl God made? The girl with dreams and plans? The one who most likely met many hurts along the way?

Did you know the things that hurt you, hurt him too? Did you know he catches your tears in a bottle? Do you realize it doesn't matter how many times you stumble and fall? He is always there, loving you.

Give your heart to him—all at once, or piece by piece, tear by tear, or wave by wave. He can work it out. He can heal you. He can set you free.

~

I once had a dream that I was standing on a stage, speaking to an audience. On a table before me were porcelain masks from my childhood collection, and there was a hammer in my hand. I began smashing the masks with the hammer. As the blows fell down on their perfect faces, they exploded and shards sprayed all over the stage. In the dream I was happy.

My dream has come true. In the writing of this book and in the speaking of my experience, I have "smashed the masks." And my Creator has lovingly, patiently, picked up every broken shard and placed them back together in a mosaic that is more beautiful than they ever were whole.

Allow me to share a glimpse of the mosaic, the life God has blessed me with.

In the quiet of the early morning, I open my eyes and see the snow falling through the pines, gathering in snowdrifts along the window-sill. I hear the sound of Shane's footsteps as he pads quietly down the hall to go upstairs, start a fire, and put on the coffee—he likes to do that before I rise, so I take a moment to linger and look at the magic falling outside my window. I will never forget setting the table for two in Munich, wanting someone to sit by my side and love me in all my imperfections, someone who would eat with me and laugh with me, someone who would love me when I was at the bottom and believe in who I could be when I rose from the ashes.

Then, God became that Someone for me. I remember when he brought Shane into my life. It was as if he realized my every need, every desire, every hope, and every dream. Each night as I lay my head on his chest, I am grateful.

Then, when our sweet daughter, Olivia, was born, it was as if God had bottled up our hopes in heaven, waiting patiently until he could pour them out for us.

Then, a couple years later, when our son, Zach, was born, it was as if God shot an arrow straight from his heart into our home.

As I lie in bed, I hear our children's voices, squealing with delight at the first snow of winter, scampering down the hallway with glee. As I linger a few moments longer, reveling in the beauty of the snow gathering on the mountain pines, I think about the joy of our family: in summertime we cannonball off our boat into the lake; in the fall we throw the football on the green fields of our yard; in the winter we make snowmen and go sledding; and in the spring we look for new blooms and ladybugs.

During breaks from writing, I walk the sunlit path along the shore of the lake, appreciating the white cranes that appear now and again over the glassy water, hobbling and then taking flight alongside me. I turn and see the tall, wide, warm home that looms in the distance. Within those walls, I will always find love, faith, a hot cup of tea, a laugh, a reprieve, and a fire.

IT'S IN THE WORD

The Bible says that Christ came to bring beauty out of ashes, to bind up the brokenhearted, to set the captives free. He takes what is broken and puts it back together as he sees fit.

These days I collect crosses. I especially love mosaics.

I even made my own mosaic cross one time. I'm not exactly *crafty*, if you know what I mean. But I am determined. So one morning during our annual trip to family camp, I went into the craft cabin, pretending to not be overwhelmed, and began picking out the tiles. I especially liked the broken-looking ones in vibrant colors. Then I took a long time arranging them in different ways on the wooden cross.

When I figured out the pattern, I thought, "OK, that's it. I'm ready to go to the lake!" But I found out I wasn't even close to being done.

Next, I had to glue on the tiles, one by one by one, turning and twisting them so they hit the light just right. "Am I done?" I asked. No. Not even close.

The next day and the next, I grouted the tiles—I had to rub cement *over* the design I worked so hard to make! Then I found out I had to sand the grout off each broken piece.

As I picked and filed and worked, my hands chapped and bled, and I thought about God's hands.

To us it is a laborious chore to put something back together and make it more beautiful than it was before we laid our hands on it. To us, it is far too much work to put back together *a life*. But to him, *it is pure joy*. "For the joy set before him [he] endured the cross" (Heb. 12:2).

You, my dear friend, who have traveled so far and so wide with me now, you are the joy. You are the delight of his heart, and it is his joy to make your mosaic.

In John 20:17, when Jesus told Mary that she couldn't hold on to him, I believe he meant that her eyes now had to shift from the temporary to the timeless, from the flesh to the spirit, from what she could see to what she could only *believe* in her heart.

Letting go of perfect is letting go of the temporary. It is fixing our eyes on the eternal. It is getting our eyes off the demands of the world and fixing them on God, the only Perfect that lasts. It is experiencing the real freedom Christ died for—freedom to be able to shrug off the imperfections, to laugh, to cultivate joy, knowing that despite this messy world, Perfect will come back for us one day and take us home, forever.

~⌒

I hung the mosaic cross on the wall in the kids' bathroom. After being baked in the fire, it came out looking pretty decent; *imperfectly beautiful*, let's say. As I straightened it on the wall, I thought, "I will never forget where I was when you found me, God."

Then I began thinking about you, my dear reader. I've wondered about you, what you would be doing right now. I've dreamt about you too. I've pictured that little girl inside of you who once ran free.

She is walking down an aisle in an old bookstore. The shelves are lined with books of many colors, both bright and dim with age. On the bottom right, the light coming in from the window draws her to this book. She picks it up and reads the title: *Girl Perfect*.

Hmm. She slumps down in the aisle and begins to read.

She is never the same.

Her life, over time, becomes a beautiful mosaic. She grows to be the girl God made. He awakens in her the purpose for which she is born. He helps her see that she can remain imperfect and be utterly loved like that.

Would it be OK if I prayed for you?

Oh, sure. Why not? It can't hurt, right?

> *Dear God, only you know my reader's heart. Only you know where her longings for perfect on Earth remain unfulfilled; only you know the areas where she is not free. You know exactly what plagues her: whether it is a perfect affirmation or acceptance; a perfect body, image, or look; a perfect dream, escape, or path; and only you know how to give her a perfect fulfillment and a perfect freedom. Fill her, Lord. Fill her and free her.*
>
> *I pray you will never let her forget this journey we've taken together and how beautiful her life can be if she puts all her desires for perfect in the palm of your able hands. Bless her and keep her and help her to walk in faith that some day, Perfect will come back for her. You, God, you are the only Perfect to be found on Earth.*
>
> *In Jesus's name, amen.*

For I wrote to you out of great distress and *anguish of heart and with many tears*, not to grieve you but to let you know *the depth of my love for you.*
— 2 Corinthians 2:4, emphasis added

The Spirit of the Sovereign Lord is on me, because…he has sent me to *bind up the brokenhearted*, to *proclaim freedom for the captives* and *release from darkness for the prisoners*…to bestow on them a crown of beauty instead of ashes, the oil of gladness instead of mourning, and a garment of praise instead of a spirit of despair.
— Isaiah 61:1–3, emphasis added

Where the *Spirit* of the Lord is, there is *freedom.*
— 2 Corinthians 3:17, emphasis added

My cup overflows. Surely *goodness and love will follow me all the days of my life*, and I will dwell in the house of the Lord forever.
— Psalm 23:5–6, emphasis added

Notes

Introduction

1. Jack London, *Martin Eden* (New York: Penguin Books, 1984), 246.

Chapter 4—The Perfect Body

1. Courtney E. Martin, *Perfect Girls, Starving Daughters: The Frightening New Normalcy of Hating Your Body* (New York: Free Press, 2007).
2. Please contact Mercy Ministries at www.mercyministries.org or Remuda Ranch at www.remudaranch.com for more information.

Chapter 5—The Perfect Look

1. London, *Martin Eden*, 246.
2. Beth Moore, *Breaking Free: Making Liberty in Christ a Reality in Life* (Nashville, TN: Lifeway Press, 1999).

Chapter 7—The Perfect Escape

1. London, *Martin Eden*, 17.

Chapter 8—The Perfect Path

1. London, *Martin Eden*, 55.
2. Robert Frost, "The Road Not Taken," Bartleby.com, http://www.bartleby.com/119/1.html (accessed May 25, 2008).

Chapter 9—The Perfect Fulfillment

1. Moore, *Breaking Free: Making Liberty in Christ a Reality in Life*, 114.
2. Ibid.

Appendix
Timeline of Jennifer Strickland's Modeling Career

Age	Location	Agency/Characters/Experiences
0–8	San Diego, CA	• Memories of a grassy backyard
8–12	Carlsbad, CA	• Took "Cinderella" class at Elegance modeling school • Did fashion shows, mannequin modeling, and photo shoots
13–16	Mission Viejo, CA	• Began doing TV commercials, including auditions for Pop-Tarts commercial • Continued fashion shows and other modeling
17	Hollywood, CA	• Signed with Nina Blanchard Agency in Los Angeles • Did her first Hollywood photo shoot • Graduated from high school • Lived with Nina in her Hollywood home for a short time before leaving for Europe
	Hamburg, Germany	• Spent the summer working in Hamburg • Shared an apartment with other models, including her Danish roommate
18	Los Angeles, CA	• Enrolled at USC • Worked in LA while going to college
	Paris, France	• Spent the first half of the summer working in Paris • Shared apartment with other models, including Victoria, a Greek *Vogue* cover model, and a Czech girl • Grabbed by man on the street • Got lost in the metro at night
	Athens, Greece	• Spent the second half of the summer working in Athens • Had the experiences of being drugged and offered a bribe to pose nude

Age	Location	Agency/Characters/Experiences
19	Los Angeles, CA	• Worked in LA while going to college • Stayed in LA for the summer and worked for Nina • Stalked by homeless man
20	Sydney, Australia	• Worked in LA while going to college • Spent the summer working in Australia • Lived with Shellie and her boyfriend Nick
	Auckland, New Zealand	• Modeled for a short period at end of summer • Traveled on her own before returning to college in fall
21	Los Angeles, CA	• Graduated college • Stayed in LA for summer, lost weight, worked out, did photo shoots, got ready for the runway in Milan
	New York, NY	• Met with Eileen Ford and signed contract with Ford Models New York • Worked in New York briefly
22	Milan, Italy	• Damien became her "unofficial" manager • Tina and Val were her roommates • Worked for Giorgio Armani • Went home for Christmas (with Bosquo) • Lost job at Armani
	Rome, Italy	• Did runway • Backpack and journal were stolen
	Siena, Italy	• Went to see American University • Met Kim, who told her about Christ
	Munich, Germany	• Lived with a lingerie model who was always gone • Contemplated suicide • Met Michael, who gave her a Bible in the park and took her to church • Traveled to *Zugspitze* and accepted Christ • Traveled to the Black Forest
	San Diego, CA	• Went home to her grassy backyard

I love the LORD, for he heard my voice;
    he heard my cry for mercy.
Because he turned his ear to me,
    I will call on him as long as I live.

                                                —PSALM 116:1–2

In addition to being a stay-at-home mom, Jennifer Strickland travels widely speaking to women and girls, encouraging them to shine from the inside out. For more information about Jennifer Strickland's ministry, to contact her about speaking at an upcoming event, and to see the ways she is impacting girls of this generation...

Visit www.jenniferstrickland.net for more information about events and resources that restore the beauty and value of women, and www.girlperfectbook.com for *The Girl Perfect Study Guide: A Journey Through the Longings of Our Hearts*, where you and your friends can study ten lies that hold you captive and ten truths that set you free.

FREE NEWSLETTERS
TO HELP EMPOWER YOUR LIFE

Why subscribe today?

☐ **DELIVERED DIRECTLY TO YOU.** All you have to do is open your inbox and read.

☐ **EXCLUSIVE CONTENT.** We cover the news overlooked by the mainstream press.

☐ **STAY CURRENT.** Find the latest court rulings, revivals, and cultural trends.

☐ **UPDATE OTHERS.** Easy to forward to friends and family with the click of your mouse.

CHOOSE THE E-NEWSLETTER THAT INTERESTS YOU MOST:

- Christian news
- Daily devotionals
- Spiritual empowerment
- And much, much more

SIGN UP AT: **http://freenewsletters.charismamag.com**

8178